FRANK H

ST STEPHEN'S GREEN

A HISTORY OF THE GREEN AND ITS ENVIRONS: THE SIGHTS, SOUNDS, CHARACTERS AND EVENTS

MERCIER PRESS

MERCIER PRESS
Cork
www.mercierpress.ie

© Text: Frank Hopkins, 2020
© Photographs: Paul Reynolds, 2020

ISBN: 978 1 78117 692 4

A CIP record for this title is available from the British Library.

Printed and bound in the EU.

CONTENTS

INTRODUCTION

This book was never intended to be a comprehensive history of St Stephen's Green, but it is my intention to give readers, both locals and visitors alike, an eclectic and entertaining flavour of events that took place in and around the streets and alleyways surrounding the Green. Hopefully this book achieves that wish. Many of the locations and features mentioned in the book, such as Harcourt Street Fields, the statue of King George II and Peg Plunkett's high-class brothel have long since disappeared, but I hope that the tales give the reader a glimpse of a little corner of Dublin that's now gone.

The Stephen's Green you'll find in these pages is not just the beautiful enclosed jewel that we all know and love today. At one time, the Green was a sprawling, marshy sixty-acre common that extended to the east as far as present-day Fitzwilliam Street, and was inhabited only by snipe shooters. It was also a place where the great and the good came, on occasion, to execute the not so great and downright bad. Numerous hangings were carried out on the Green from as early as the mid-sixteenth century; these weren't discontinued until the 1780s.

Along with the hangings, there were frequent riots. In fact, there was no better place for a dust-up in Dublin in the eighteenth and nineteenth centuries than the Green. It was the venue for a serious riot in 1700, when the weavers of the Liberties met the butchers of Dublin to settle their differences with a football match. The game never took place. Instead, the two sides fought a pitched battle leading to the deaths of at least half a dozen of the protagonists. On another occasion, in 1878, there was an intense riot in the environs of the Green when a detachment of the Wicklow Royal Artillery ran amok; this led to Harcourt Street being closed down for hours.

In addition to tales of the bishops, lords and ladies who inhabited the magnificent houses bordering St Stephen's Green, there are also the less-than-salubrious stories of the huddled masses who lived in the warren of narrow streets and alleyways just behind the west side of the Green and the Royal College of Surgeons. The infamous Goat Alley, for example, was a den of iniquity and possibly one of Dublin's most dangerous streets during the eighteenth century. It was home to many of the city's brothels, and a large number of Dublin's graverobbing fraternity operated from there – mainly due to its proximity to the Royal College, where the young surgeons needed a steady supply of bodies on which to practise their trade.

There is also a wealth of fascinating stories to be found

in the areas surrounding Stephen's Green. Close by were Harcourt Street Fields – now Harcourt Street, the home of the world-famous Copper Face Jacks nightclub and the centre of Dublin's bustling club scene. Back in the day, Harcourt Street Fields were a lawless place 'where no decent woman could walk', as one unnamed scribe put it, and where violence and outrage were the order of the day.[1]

In the same vein, the nearby Mercer Street Upper was once known as French Street, but the name was changed in the mid-eighteenth century, as C. T. McCready puts it in his *Dublin Street Names, Dated and Explained*, 'on account of previous bad repute'.[2] Before Dublin's famous 'Monto' came into existence on the city's northside, the main red-light district was largely based around French Street.

Immediately to the south of the Green, and originally bordering Harcourt Street Fields, lies one of Dublin's hidden gems: the Iveagh Gardens. This was once Copper-faced Jack's private garden (the real-life figure, not the nightclub!) and later became the Coburg Gardens (before reverting to the original name in the late nineteenth century), where you might have found activities ranging from a political riot to a ten-mile race over hurdles between a man and a horse called Rover. One of the features of the gardens – the long, sunken archery pit where Ireland's first female sports superstar Cecilia Betham plied her trade – can still be seen there.

The book wouldn't be complete without the larger-than-life characters who lived or worked in the environs of the Green, such as the likes of Harcourt residents Leonard McNally, the infamous informer, and Bram Stoker, author of one of the world's bestselling books, *Dracula*. Another horror classic, *Melmoth the Wanderer*, was penned by Charles Maturin, who lived just a stone's throw away on York Street.

Some of the lesser-known characters who appear include the bodysnatcher and Goat Alley resident Michael Farrell and his near neighbour Fanny Stuart, who ran a notorious 'house of ill-fame'. At the other end of that scale, in what is now Balfe Street, we have Peg Plunkett, otherwise known as Margaret Leeson, who ran the city's best high-class brothel, which was frequented by bankers, politicians and even the lord lieutenant of Ireland.

The vast bulk of the research material for the book was sourced in contemporary newspapers, and, as usual, I am indebted to the legions of long-dead and unnamed scribes who wrote down the stories in the first place. I am also greatly indebted to Paul Reynolds for the pictures he so kindly took for this book.

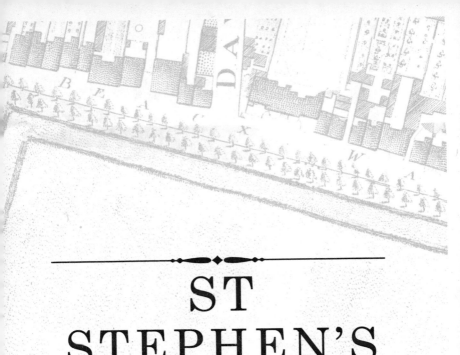

ST
STEPHEN'S
GREEN

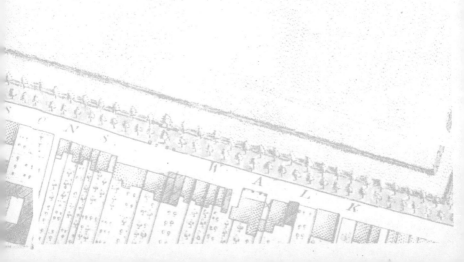

THE GREEN

A Brief History

To most people today, St Stephen's Green, the jewel in the crown of Dublin's Office of Public Works, is the beautiful Victorian park enclosed by railings in the centre of the city. However, in order to get a proper sense of the Green, it is important to dig deeper into its history.

The Green was once part of a floodplain of the ancient Steyne River and was a rough marshy wasteland comprised of about sixty acres on the edge of Dublin city. It takes its name from its connection with the church of St Stephen, which stood roughly on the site where Mercer's Medical Centre is now located. In the thirteenth century, St Stephen's was described as a church with a leper hospital attached.

The Green is first mentioned in a document called *Liber Albus* in Latin or *The White Book of the City of Dublin*. In 1236 the mayor and corporation of Dublin granted Robert Fitz Nicholas a piece of land known as 'le Rath' that was:

[W]estward to the land of the Nuns of the Blessed Virgin Mary at Hogges; northward towards Steyn; eastward to the Dodir and the meadow of Richard Olof; southward, to the road from Dublin to Donachbrok, and to the meadow of the Archbishop of Dublin, and to the city's common pasture called the Green area of St Stephen, towards the north, and, towards the west, to the land of the aforesaid nuns.[1]

It was also mentioned in the calendar that 'on Thursday after the festival of the Nativity of St. John the Baptist, [June 24] 1329 …', Adam and Geoffrey Craddock and others unknown were charged in court with going into a woman's house in Dublin, where they took Ralph of Mestoun against his will and 'led him so far as the Green of St Stephen, in the suburb of the city, and there beat him in violation of the King's peace'.[2]

In 1635 the assembly of Dublin decreed that the common areas of the city be kept for the use of the citizens:

That no parsel of the Greenes or commons of the city shall henceforth be lett, but wholie kept for the use of the citizens and others to walke and take open aire, by this this cittie is at present groweing very populous.[3]

However, by 1663 the city's coffers were empty and the city assembly came up with a plan to sell plots of land at

Stephen's Green and other areas of wasteland in order to raise money. The Dublin Assembly Roll for that year states:

> *Whereas certaine of the commons petitioned unto the said assembly, sheweing that they are very sensible how that by reason of the late rebellion and longe continued troubles of this kingdome the threasury of this cittie is cleerly exhausted and the yearly revenue is reduced to little or nothing, soe that in all likelyhood they will not be able to defray the publique chardge which must of necessitie fall on them, if not tymely prevented by the said assembly; therefore the said commons prayed the said assembly to lay downe a course whereby the revenue of the said cittie may be increased, and that the said assembly would be pleased that some or all of these followeing propositions may be made use of towards the effecting of soe good a worke: first, that the out skerts of Saint Stephen's Greene and other wast lands about this cittie, that now addeth nothing att all to pleasure or profitt, may be sett for ninetie nine years, or to fee farm, and a considerable rent reserved ...*[4]

A survey was carried out by Captain Robert Newcomen and, based on his findings, it was decided that seventeen acres of the Green would be set out for rental. This happened the following year, in 1664, when eighty-six parcels of land were let out. Would-be buyers had to draw lots for the right to rent a plot from the city; the first tenants were a collection of merchants, aldermen, tailors, bakers and other Dublin tradesmen and professionals.

The Green as we know it was walled in and gated by 1666. As part of this renovation, it was 'levelled and made smooth' so that it could be used by 'his majesties horse and foot guards' and the city militia to exercise in.[5]

Despite all this work, by the late eighteenth century Stephen's Green was in a deplorable state and had become something of a convenient dumping ground. All manner of refuse was disposed of in the ditches surrounding it. There were many complaints regarding the condition of the Green during that period, but surely this complaint from an anonymous gentleman to the editor of the *Hibernian Journal* in February 1773 was one of the strangest:

> *Gentlemen, Invited by a remarkable fine morning, on Wednesday last, to take a turn in St. Stephen's Green, I was no less interrupted than astonished at the remarkable appearance of two servant men, without hats, in blue liveries faced with yellow, who had taken their station about the tenth hour, in that part of the Gravel Walk that is opposite the end of Hume Street, for the purpose of striking a large dirty carpet, from whence arose such repeated clouds of dust, as totally to prevent the usual course of passengers, to the no small entertainment of the motley performers, who continued their exercise while there remained any sport in view, or ammunition to annoy the enemy.*
>
> *Trifling as the above offence may seem, should it become a practice, it might prove a nuisance of such a serious nature;*

to prevent which, induced me to be thus officious; differing in opinion from the vulgar and indolent, who think what is every one's business, is nobody's.

I am, Gentlemen, Your Constant Reader, And the Public's humble Servant.

SOMEBODY[6]

In late October 1781 the body of a small boy was found in a ditch at Stephen's Green near Leeson's Walk and an inquest subsequently found that the child had been wilfully murdered by 'some person, or persons unknown'.[7]

Two years later, the Dublin authorities were making efforts to clean up the Green by building embankments around the ditches, and the *Hibernian Journal* reported:

The [building of the] embankment of the ditches in Stephen's Green, after having been discontinued for some years, is resumed, insomuch that the North or Beaux Walk, will be completed this summer, exhibiting the pleasing object of a handsome canal, instead of a muddy weed-grown ditch.[8]

Despite this, the decline of the Green continued apace. During and after the tumultuous period of the 1798 rebellion that was launched by the United Irishmen – a revolutionary republican organisation, formed in Belfast, which was inspired by the American Revolution and aligned with French revolutionaries – the Green was made constant use of by the military, meaning that the one-time jewel in the crown of Dublin city's parklands became a hideous mess.

Matters began to improve in 1814 after the residents of St Stephen's Green agitated for improvements. The Green was effectively privatised through an Act of Parliament and commissioners took over the running of the park. The old wall that had been erected in the seventeenth century was demolished and all the surrounding ditches were filled in. The park was also drained and levelled, and old trees and shrubs were cleared and new ones planted. A set of railings was erected around the boundary.

Once these improvements were finalised, only local residents who paid a fee had access to the park. There was a great deal of anger at the decision to close the Green to the public, however, resulting in many protests. These protests rumbled on sporadically for another sixty years until 1876, when Sir Arthur Guinness, MP for Dublin, offered to pay the commissioners to reopen the park to the public. When his offer was accepted, Guinness also paid for a total makeover of the Green. With his money, and under his guidance, the park was transformed into the gem that we all know and love today.

HANGINGS
AT THE GREEN

———————◆———————

SITE OF THE GALLOWS

One of the less savoury aspects of the Green was that, for many years, it was a place where members of Dublin's criminal fraternity were taken to be executed.

Although many hangings were recorded as having taken place in the vicinity of St Stephen's Green, it is likely that none actually took place on the Green as we know it today. It is hard to pinpoint the exact position of the gallows as, when recording these events, most eighteenth- and nineteenth-century newspapers gave the location as simply 'at' or 'near' St Stephen's Green. One double execution reported in the *Dublin Intelligencer* took place 'beyond' St Stephen's Green. This happened on 15 December 1711 and the people hanged were a man named McDonnell, who had been convicted of robbery, and a man named Gorman, who was executed for murdering a girl.[9]

The most likely spot was in or around the crossroads of

the current Lower Baggot Street and Fitzwilliam Street, though it is possible – but by no means certain – that the gallows was at least sometimes placed at the corner of the Green closest to Harcourt Street.

In his *Reminiscences of an Emigrant Milesian*, Andrew O'Reilly described the place of execution:

> *At that period capital sentences were carried into execution on a gibbet erected a little behind the spot on which the corner houses of Fitzwilliam Street and Baggot Street now stand, as you proceed towards the canal bridge. I remember a pool of water then filling the remains, I think, of an excavation called the Gallows Quarry; but the place on which the instrument of execution was, was known as Gallows Green, called, from its vicinity to it, but improperly, Stephen's Green, from which it was distant several hundred yards.*[10]

In his famous Gothic novel *The Cock and Anchor*, set in Dublin, Joseph Sheridan Le Fanu describes the execution of the fictional character of Sir Henry Ashwoode at the Green:

> *The place of public execution for criminals was then, and continued to be for long after, a spot significantly denominated 'Gallows Hill,' situated in the neighbourhood of St Stephen's Green, and not far from the line at present traversed by*

Baggot Street. There a permanent gallows was erected, and thither, at length, amid thousands of crowding spectators, the melancholy procession came, and proceeded to the centre of the area, where the gallows stood, with the long new rope swinging in the wind, and the cart and the hangman, with the guard of soldiers, prepared for their reception. The vehicles drew up, and those who had a part to play in the dreadful scene descended. The guard took their place, preserving a narrow circle around the fatal spot, free from the pressure of the crowd. The carriages were driven a little away, and the coffin was placed under the gallows, while Ashwoode, leaning upon the chaplain and upon one of the sheriffs, proceeded toward the cart, which made the rude platform on which he was to stand. ...

It was said, that Mr. Blarden, the prosecutor, was in a house in Stephen's Green, to see the hanging, and as soon as the mob heard it, they went and broke the windows, and, but for the soldiers, would have forced their way in, and done more violence.[11]

Even though *The Cock and Anchor* is a work of fiction, it seems highly likely that Le Fanu was drawing on real-life Dublin geography, as well as his own family's history, to describe the scene. (An ancestor of Le Fanu's was the prosecutor in a case against a Dublin servant named Oliver Deacon, who was hanged at the Green in 1747. More detail on this case will be given later in the chapter.)

A note in *The Irish Times* from October 1927 says, in relation to the location of the gallows: 'It may be added that in Baggot Street, Lower, it was a quarry, on the site of which now stands Rock Lane, and opposite was the site of the gallows.'[12]

Another reference to the gallows, in *The Freeman's Journal* in 1764, refers to a 'deep-yawning and fenceless quarry that undermines the high Road that stands near the Gallows that stands near Stephen's Green'.[13]

Further evidence that the gallows was located around that area is seen in this newspaper report of 1756:

> *In the evening, a boy about eleven years old riding a high spirited horse, he took fright near the gallows and run away with him, and near Bagatrot Castle [located at the junction of Lower Baggot Street and Waterloo Road], he was thrown, and received much hurt that 'tis feared he will not recover.*[14]

It has also been said that an area somewhere close to the College of Surgeons had a gallows, but there is not much evidence to support this notion. This was the last part of the area surrounding Stephen's Green to be developed and it was notorious for its lawlessness. One writer said that this area had a bad reputation not only because of the Huguenot graveyard:

> *but because it had been a site for public executions; a young*
> *girl, Mary Creighton, was executed here in 1729 for stealing*
> *a calico gown. Further, it bordered on a poorer part of the city*
> *and had been known as the Rapparee Fields, a hideout for*
> *robbers and footpads.*[15]

Regardless of the exact location of the gallows, it is certain that it was located very close to the Green, and this, without doubt, adds a ghoulish dimension to the area's history, as it is beyond contention that many executions, both mundane and notorious, took place there over the centuries.

EXECUTIONS

One of the earliest known executions at or around the Green was that of the archbishop of Cashel, Dermot O'Hurley, who was executed in 1584. O'Hurley was born at Lycadoon in Co. Limerick and received his education on the continent at Louvain, where he became a professor of philosophy. He also studied law at Reims and held a professorship of law at that institute. He later went to Rome and in 1581 was appointed archbishop of Cashel by Pope Gregory XIII.

Because of the penal laws then in force in Ireland, laws that made it difficult for Catholics to practise their religion, the archbishop was forced to return to Ireland secretly in order to avoid capture by Queen Elizabeth's spies at Dublin Castle. Heavily disguised, he landed at Skerries in 1583 and quickly made his way to Waterford. However, Elizabeth's spies had intercepted his letters and were actively seeking him.

O'Hurley hid for a time at Slane Castle with the Baron of Slane. From there he made his way to Carrick-on-Suir, where he expected to come under the protection of the Earl of Ormond. Meanwhile, the two lord justices – Henry Wallop and Adam Loftus, the Protestant archbishop of Dublin – discovered that Baron Slane had sheltered O'Hurley and threatened him with dire personal consequences if he didn't deliver O'Hurley to them immediately.

Faced with the prospect of being arrested himself, the baron sped off to Carrick-on-Suir, where he apprehended the archbishop and took him back to Dublin Castle. Upon being questioned by the lord justices, O'Hurley admitted to being a Roman Catholic but refused to answer any other questions. In an effort to make him recant his faith, or at least inform on other leading Catholics such as the Earl of Kildare, Thomas Walsingham, Queen Elizabeth's secretary, ordered that the archbishop be subjected to a torture known as 'The Boots'.

The historian Richard Stanihurst has described this gruesome torture: in the castle yard, before the officials of the government, the executioner placed the archbishop's feet and calves in tin boots filled with oil. His feet were then fastened in wooden shackles or stocks, and fire was placed under them. When the oil reached boiling point, it so penetrated the feet and legs that morsels of skin and flesh fell off and left the bones bare.

Despite this gruesome torture, the archbishop resisted all attempts to make him renounce his faith, so he was brought back to his cell in the Bermingham Tower at Dublin Castle. He remained there until sometime in June 1584. Two days before the end of their tenure as lords justices, Wallop and Loftus decided to try the archbishop for treason. He was court-martialled and sentenced to death.

On the morning of 21 June 1584 he was taken from the castle and brought to the scaffold at the Green, where he was hanged in front of two townspeople and a friend of the archbishop named Fitzsimons. His body was said to have been thrown into a ditch near the gallows. Later that night, under the cover of darkness, Fitzsimons and some other friends of the archbishop took his remains and buried him in the little churchyard of St Kevin in Camden Row. For many years afterwards the grave was a place of pilgrimage for the Catholics of Dublin; today no trace of the burial plot remains.

In his book *Life in Old Dublin*, James Collins said:

The martyr was hanged in St. Stephen's Green, then outside the city. The Green was then an osiery, and in order to prolong his agony his three executioners hanged him with a rope made of twigs. The site of the scaffold was, according to tradition, where Fitzwilliam Street crosses Baggot Street, where executions took place up to a comparatively late date. This place was known as Gallows Road in 1756.[16]

***

The next hanging that we know took place at or near St Stephen's Green was that of John Atherton, bishop of Waterford and Lismore. In December 1640 Atherton was tried and convicted for engaging in the act of sodomy with his steward, John Childe.

John Atherton was born in Somerset, England, in 1598. He was a member of a wealthy English family and received his education at Oxford University. Shortly after leaving Oxford, he became a rector in the Church of England and served as prebendary of St John's in Dublin and chancellor of Christ Church. He came to the attention of Thomas Wentworth, Earl of Strafford and lord lieutenant of Ireland, who appointed him bishop of Waterford in 1636.

Atherton appeared in court in 1640 and strongly denied the charge against him. However, Childe gave evidence against him, and the bishop was condemned to death. It is ironic that Atherton was one of the first men to receive the death sentence for the crime of sodomy, as he had been a leading advocate in the campaign to make homosexual acts punishable by death.

The bishop was sentenced to die on Friday 27 November and was taken to Dublin Castle to await execution. There were several sensationalist accounts written about the case afterwards, including one pamphlet that falsely claimed that he had been charged with bestiality and 'uncleanness with a cow and other creatures'. Another contemporary publication made the claim that he had been convicted for 'incest, buggery and many other enormous crimes'.[17]

Although Atherton had pleaded not guilty to the charge in court, he decided that the sanctity of the churchyard would be too good for his remains and asked the clerk of St John's church and the verger of Christ Church to allow him to be buried under a rubbish heap in a corner of St John's churchyard near Fishamble Street.

Full of remorse, Atherton attributed his downfall to:

'[The] reading of bad books, viewing of immodest pictures, frequenting of plays, drunkenness etc.' and he refused to accept Communion as he considered himself unworthy of the sacrament. He also decided at one point that 'a dog's death was too good for him' and considered asking to be beheaded instead of hanged.[18]

On the morning of the bishop's execution, he was taken in a coach to the gallows at St Stephen's Green. He was escorted by two city sheriffs and the county sheriff 'with a great company of halberds [swordsmen] to assist him'.[19] As the grim procession made its way past Christ Church, the 'passing-bell' was tolled. One eyewitness – Nicholas Bernard, dean of Ardagh – said that he had never seen either the town or the castle so crowded before.

The sheriff ordered that the bishop's arms be secured with a 'three-penny cord as a common felon' for the journey, a detail that seemed to enrage Bernard, who objected to the bishop being treated as a 'common rogue' in this manner.[20]

When he had completed his last speech at the foot of the gallows, Atherton climbed the ladder and placed his head in the noose. His hands were untied and he was allowed to fasten a handkerchief over his face. According to Bernard:

> When he had sung the 51st and the 38th Psalms, and closed with Psalm the 116th, he kneeled and prayed, and having given some Money to the Executioner, and gave him a sign when he would be ready, he took hold of his Canonical Coat near the Skirts, least he should seem to struggle at going off, and dy'd very soon.[21]

Atherton was left hanging for nearly an hour, after which his corpse was taken down for burial that night in St John's churchyard, as he had requested. John Childe was executed shortly afterwards on the bridge of Bandon in Co. Cork.

***

Women were also often led to the gallows. Sarah Grew from Loughgall in Co. Armagh was hanged at St Stephen's Green on 13 July 1717 for several thefts and for receiving stolen goods. Her father was a notorious highwayman and he himself was hanged when Sarah was only a child.

Sarah had arrived in Dublin sometime around 1710 and worked as a servant at various addresses in James's Street, Patrick Street, High Street and Vicar Street. She also appears to have worked as a prostitute on the side. In a broadside published by the quack doctor John Whalley at the time of her execution, it was stated that Sarah lived for a time with a William Constable in High Street, where she 'behav'd herself with the utmost Insolence and Impudence, and not without Suspicion of Theft and Whoredom …'[22]

Sarah was eventually convicted for stealing goods worth around £200 from a Mrs Webb, who had employed her for a few years. Sarah initially tried to place the blame for the robberies on Mrs Webb's daughter, then withdrew the charge on the eve of her execution, only to then change her story again at the last minute.[23]

A number of other robberies were taken into consideration at her trial, many of which took place in Arundal Court, where the publisher John Whalley lived. He was particularly vindictive in his condemnation of her. Hanging Sarah clearly wasn't enough of a punishment in his eyes and he rounded off his broadside with a withering denunciation of the condemned woman:

> [N]o Body that knows Mrs. Webb or her Daughter, will give Credit to any Callumnies rais'd against them by a notorious Thief and Whore, under Condemnation for her Crimes. And if I am not miss-inform'd by the Chyrurgeon that Cured her, the condemn'd Miscreant was Poxt twice, and Miscarry'd in Dublin twice, and upon that Account left her last Service, to have the Opportunity for so doing, without Suspition.[24]

When a woman was sentenced to death in Ireland during the eighteenth century, she could apply to the court to have her sentence commuted if she could prove that she was pregnant. This was known in common parlance as 'pleading her belly'. One woman who refused to do this was Dublin woman Mary Costelloe, who, along with her husband Edward, was hanged at St Stephen's Green for doctoring coins. It was reported in the newspapers on

14 July 1750 that, after the judge had passed the death sentence, Mary Costelloe refused to 'plead her belly', saying that she would rather die in the arms of her husband.

Another figure who was hanged on this gallows was the famous Dublin brothel-keeper named Darky or Dorcas Kelly, after whom Darkey Kelly's pub in Fishamble Street is named. Kelly was the madam of an infamous brothel in Copper Alley when she was convicted of the murder of a cobbler named John Dowling on 7 January 1761. She was partially hanged and then burned at or near the Green. The barbaric practice of burning malefactors was rarely seen in Ireland, though, when it was, it was usually reserved for women. After the execution, her friends took her remains back to Newgate Prison – where she had been incarcerated – to be waked, but were refused entry. She was then taken to Copper Alley for a send-off and buried at Merrion churchyard on the southside of the city.

***

Regardless of gender, descriptions of executions at the Stephen's Green gallows are few and far between. However, we do have an interesting description of one that took place on 21 June 1727. A newspaper report describes the death procession of a Dublin surgeon from George's Lane named John Audouin (also spelled Odwin), who was hanged for murder at the Green that year.

Audouin was a French surgeon who had been convicted of the murder of his maid, Margaret Kief. It was alleged that Audouin had forced himself on her and when she resisted he killed her and cut up her body. The main witness against him at his trial was John Turner, a shoe boy who had been hiding in the coal cellar on the night of the murder. Although the dead woman's clothes and Audouin's bloody shirt were found concealed at the surgeon's house, the surgeon went to the gallows denying that he had any part in the crime.

On the day of his execution, Audouin was taken from his prison cell at Newgate and paraded through the city at one o'clock. He was said to have been relaxed as he waved to his friends in the streets on his way to Stephen's Green. His arms were untied and he stood up in the cart, leaning on his oak coffin, which he had chosen himself. Throughout the journey he read from a prayer book and, on reaching the gallows near Stephen's Green, he prayed and addressed the assembled crowd for over two-and-a-half hours. When he had said all that he had to say, Audouin put the noose around his own neck. Spotting one of those who had given evidence against him in the crowd, he begged for the man to be brought forward so that he could forgive him. Audouin embraced the man, said a few more words and, according to the reporter, 'stretched forth his arms and cried, Lord Jesus have mercy on my soul, suddenly closed his hands and sprung from the cart, with such force, that he never moved more'.[25]

***

The gallows also, occasionally, proved to have different uses. In June 1735, for example, it was reported that weavers from the Liberties in Dublin had hung calico from the gallows at Stephen's Green in a protest at the importation of cheaper calico from India. Earlier that day, they had dressed two effigies in calico and drew them in a cart to a gallows in the Liberties, where they hanged them in a mock ceremony.[26] Six years earlier, weavers from the nearby St Kevin's Port dug up the gallows on St Stephen's Green. This was during a riot with the police, in which one of the weavers was killed.

Still, the gallows was mostly used for its primary purpose. In early December 1747, for example, a servant named Oliver Deacon was convicted at the Dublin Quarter Sessions for robbing his master, Mr Le Fanu, at his house on Stephen's Green. The court heard that Deacon had used a skeleton key to steal sums of money from his master's safe on several occasions. Once found guilty, he was sentenced to death.

Deacon was hanged at Stephen's Green on 23 December, but that wasn't the end of the matter. It sometimes happened after a hanging that the executed criminal's family and friends would take the hanged man's corpse and lay it at the front door of the accuser. That's what happened in this case.

On 29 December, the *Dublin Courant* reported that, after the hanging, and led by John Deacon of the Ormond Market, brother of the hanged man, a mob of:

> *several vagrant and wicked rabble assembled most riotously in a tumultuous manner at Mr Lefanue's [sic] house at Stephen's Green, where they laid the corpse of the malefactor, broke the windows, pulled up the rails, and endeavoured forcibly to enter into the said house which they would have done had the main guard not come and prevented them.*[27]

Rioting was a fairly common occurrence in Dublin at that time, but this must have been an exceptional one, as the lord lieutenant placed a bounty of £30 – a huge sum at that time – on John Deacon's head, and £20 for anyone else involved in the riot. It is not known if Deacon or any of his companions were ever caught.

***

One of the most famous hangings to take place at Stephen's Green was that of four pirates: George Gidley, Andreas Zekerman, Richard St Quintin and Peter McKinley, which took place in early March 1766.

A few months earlier, in November 1765, the men – all sailors – had been serving on board the *Earl of Sandwich*, which was bound for London from the Canary Islands with a rich cargo of gold, jewellery and Spanish dollars. The four men took over the ship, killing the commander, John Cochrane, and his partner, George Glas, as well as Glas's wife and daughter, who were thrown over the side by McKinley.

The men set sail for the south coast of Ireland, where they scuttled the ship near Duncannon Fort in Co. Wexford. Having killed the remaining crew, the four men made their way ashore in a longboat with as much of the ship's treasure as they could carry. They came ashore on 3 December 1765 with an estimated 250 bags of Spanish dollars, along with bags of gold dust and a huge haul of jewellery, which they buried on the beach at Duncannon.

The men then went on a drunken spree in New Ross. They bought horses and pistols and spent so much money that they soon attracted the attention of the authorities, who suspected they were pirates. Suspicions deepened further when the wreck of the *Earl of Sandwich* was blown ashore soon afterwards.

Looking to avoid arrest, the men decided to head to Dublin, where they stayed at the Black Bull Tavern in Thomas Street. Their plan failed, however, and they were arrested and lodged in Newgate Prison. On 1 March

1766 they were found guilty of robbery and murder and sentenced to death. Two days later they were taken under military escort to Stephen's Green, where they were hanged.

The bodies were taken to Ringsend, where they were hanged in chains as a warning to others. They were later removed to a place called Muglins Island after complaints from the public about the offensive sight and smell. The bodies were displayed hanging from a gallows on the island, where they could easily be seen from passing ships.

**

Not all the executions went according to plan. *The Freeman's Journal* of 10 August 1775 reported on the almost farcical execution of William Wardell at St Stephen's Green. Wardell had been sentenced to death for stealing a considerable amount of jewellery and silver from the home of Lady Parsons. Before the execution, Wardell got up in front of the crowd and said his last few words. He was said to have 'behaved with a contrition and decency befitting his unfortunate situation'.

Wardell stepped up to the gallows, as did the new rookie hangman, who – instead of making the usual noose – proceeded to wind the rope around the condemned man's neck 'in an awkward bungling manner'. The day was only saved when a member of the crowd, who had witnessed many executions, stepped forward to show the new man how things were done, and poor Wardell was dispatched, said *The Freeman's Journal*, 'according to the rules of art'.[28]

***

As the eighteenth century wore on, executions at the Green became more unruly and were often attended by violence as friends and families of the hanged tussled with the authorities to get the bodies of their loved ones back.

Take the execution of James Craddock, who was convicted of being a Whiteboy (a member of a secret agrarian society, formed to protect the rights of small tenant farmers) and for the murder of a man named Ambrose Power in Co. Tipperary in 1778. As was the practice, Craddock was taken from Newgate in a cart across the city to be hanged and quartered at Stephen's Green under a strong military guard.

The hanging part of the sentence was carried out but, as the hangman was beginning to cut up the corpse of the unfortunate man, a riot broke out. The immense crowd, who were sympathetic to the dead man, began stoning the soldiers and the hangman. The hangman was badly injured and had his skull fractured along with many other injuries. Fortunately for him, his comrades made good use of the death cart, loading him into it and taking him back to Newgate in an unconscious state along with two of the rioters.[29]

Having family and friends in the crowd could also come in handy in other ways. On 24 November 1781 Dubliner Thomas Lonergan (named Lanigan by some newspapers) was 'turned off' at the gallows for the murder of his employer Captain Thomas O'Flaherty at Castlefield in Co. Kilkenny. Again, the question of exactly where the execution took place arises. Some reports state that it was Baggot Street, while contemporary newspaper reports say that it took place 'at' or 'near' the Green.

Lonergan had been employed by Captain O'Flaherty and his wife, Susannah, as a tutor to their sons at their home in Kilkenny in 1776. This was an arrangement that worked out just fine until Lonergan and the captain's wife fell in love. The lovers decided at some point to do away with Captain O'Flaherty and Lonergan felt that the best way to achieve this was by poisoning him.

Over a period of time, he visited several apothecaries in the area, buying just enough arsenic from each one 'to kill the rats' at Castlefield. The couple then put phase two of the plan into action. One evening they laced the captain's dinner with a liberal dose of arsenic. And just 'to be sure, to be sure', they put another generous helping of the lethal substance into the captain's custard dessert.

Needless to say, the captain went to bed that night

in terrible pain and died in agony some time later. The local doctor was called to examine the body, but, despite the evidence of swelling and black spots on the body, he certified that O'Flaherty had died from natural causes.

The captain was buried soon afterwards and for a while it seemed that Lonergan and Mrs O'Flaherty would get away with their crime. Lonergan continued to live in the family home. About one year after the captain's death, however, Mrs O'Flaherty had a quarrel with her sixteen-year-old son John and cut off his allowance. He retaliated by going to the authorities, telling them of his suspicion that his father had been poisoned. An investigation was launched, and although nothing could be proved against them, Lonergan and Susannah O'Flaherty panicked and went on the run.

While in hiding, Susannah convinced Lonergan to give himself up to the magistrates and stand trial, telling him that he was sure to be acquitted. Lonergan was at first dubious about this proposition, but he changed his mind when his partner in crime promised him that she too would give herself up at a later date. Thus reassured, Lonergan surrendered to a Gowran magistrate and on 28 June 1778 was promptly charged as follows:

> [That] not having the fear of God before his eyes, nor the duty of his allegiance considering, but being moved and seduced by the

instigation of the Devil [he] did traitorously kill and murder Thomas O'Flaherty.[30]

Once the authorities had their man in custody, they didn't look too hard for Mrs O'Flaherty and she took the opportunity to flee the country, leaving Lonergan to face the music alone.

Lonergan's trial took place at the Court of the King's Bench in Dublin on 19 November 1781. The principal witness against him was O'Flaherty's son, John, who gave evidence that his mother and Lonergan had become very familiar in the months leading up to his father's death. He also stated that he and his sister had become violently ill after mistakenly eating a small portion of their father's dinner on the evening of his death and had been severely punished for their error.

Despite his protestations of innocence, Lonergan was found guilty of the murder of Captain O'Flaherty and was sentenced to be hanged and quartered on the gallows at Baggot Street. The sentence was duly carried out two days later, on 21 November.

The *Hibernian Journal* reported that 300 members of the Dublin Volunteer Corps escorted Lonergan's execution cart across Dublin to the scaffold on horseback and on foot. Lonergan made his last speech, in which he denied any involvement in the killing of O'Flaherty, and was then hanged. It was reported afterwards that his body was left dangling on the scaffold for about twenty minutes before it was cut down and handed over to Lonergan's family for burial. The quartering element of the sentence wasn't carried out on this occasion. Writing many years after the execution, Dublin magistrate Frank Thorpe Porter said that his father, who had attended the execution, told him that the city sheriff:

> *handed a sharp penknife to the executioner, who made two incisions across each other on the back of the neck. This was considered a formal compliance with the portion of the sentence which directed 'quartering'.*[31]

According to some reports, Lonergan's friends and family saw that he was still breathing and rushed him to a nearby house, where they managed to revive him by rubbing his neck and pouring brandy down his throat. Against all the odds, Lonergan slowly came back to the land of the living. He had cheated the hangman. His family then reportedly filled his coffin with stones and carried it to Kilmainham, where they proceeded with a mock funeral in the graveyard at Bully's Acre. Other reports say that the burial place was at Kilbarrack in north County Dublin.

The deception only worked for a short while, however, and news of Lonergan's amazing escape from death soon became public knowledge. Lonergan decided that he didn't want to give the Dublin public a repeat performance on the gallows. He fled to London and from there to France, where it was said that he ended his days in a Trappist monastery.

***

The last man to be hanged at St Stephen's Green was Patrick Dougherty, in 1782. He was sentenced to death for robbing a wine merchant named Thomas Moran on Ormond Quay. Moran was on his way home late on 13 August when he was attacked by five armed men, who robbed him of a gold watch, his shoes and a pair of silver buckles.[32]

A few weeks later, in October, Moran recognised Dougherty as one of the gang who had robbed him and had him arrested. As it turned out, Dougherty was the leader of a major gang that had been responsible for many robberies in the city. Dougherty was hanged at noon on 21 December 1782. Afterwards, his body was cut down from the gallows and his friends seized it, intending to lay it at the door of the wine merchant who had accused him of theft.

Bearing the body of their dead comrade aloft, the mob proceeded towards Bachelors Walk:

> *[in] a tumultuous and riotous manner towards the accuser's house but they were stopped by a party of volunteers in Abbey Street who arrested the ringleaders. The volunteers seized Dougherty's body and brought it to Trinity College for dissection, but the dead man's friends again intervened and were eventually given back the body on the condition that it would be buried without further delay and without any further disturbance of the peace.*[33]

The public were thoroughly fed up with these displays and it was rumoured in Dublin that a group of citizens had vowed to take direct action if there were any more attempts to lay the corpse of a criminal at their accuser's door. Some even threatened to seize the bodies and publicly burn them.

It was incidents like this one that persuaded the city authorities that they needed to exert more control over public hangings. Soon afterwards, the lord lieutenant of Ireland ordered that, in future, all executions were to be carried out in front of Newgate Prison, where there would be no need for a procession across the city and where prisoners could be hanged securely within the confines of the gaol. At the same time, the public could still witness the 'turning off' of criminals, but there would at least be no more battles between relatives and authorities to gain control of the bodies afterwards. In addition, it was felt that a hanging high up over the front door of Newgate made for a far greater spectacle and would make a deeper impression on any wannabe criminals who happened to be looking on:

We are informed, that in order to strike a terror into criminals, his Excellency the Lord Lieutenant has given orders, that convicts shall in future be hanged at the prison door [Newgate Prison], instead of the usual place of execution. This, it is imagined, will be a more effectual means of deterring the practices of murder and robbery, than any other mode hitherto thought of, as the parade of bringing unhappy wretches through a city, amid the sighs, and too often the commendation, pity, and tears of the common people, mitigated the horrors of such an untimely end, and made many of them plunge into eternity in the false asseveration of their innocence, to increase the compassion of the mistaken multitude.[34]

However, while Dougherty was the last man to be hanged on Stephen's Green, he wasn't the last person to be executed there. That dubious title goes to a woman named Mary Fairfield (sometimes called Catherine Fairfield) who was strangled and burned there in 1784. Although executions had been moved to Newgate Prison on the north side of the Liffey, the city authorities made an exception in Fairfield's case. It is not known why they deviated from the standard practice, but for some reason it was decided to make a very public example of her:

> *Yesterday Funt the Constable, and Catherine Fairfield, received sentence of death at the commission of Oyer and Terminer, for the inhuman murder of a poor woman, whose only defence against them was demanding her wages for nursing a child. The circumstances of this barbarous affair are too shocking to relate.*[35]

She was convicted in October 1783, along with the deceased's husband, named only as Constable Funt. After conviction, Fairfield had 'pleaded her belly' and, after being examined by a jury of matrons, she was given a respite. She made the same plea in February and July, but when it became clear that she wasn't actually pregnant, the court decided to go ahead with her punishment:

> *Monday Mary Fairfield, who was tried and convicted last October commission for the murder of Mary Burne, but pleaded pregnancy, received sentence in his Majesty's Court of King's Bench, to be executed on Saturday the 7th of August.*[36]

On the day of the execution, the procession from Newgate to Stephen's Green was described as 'awful and conducted with that solemnity which impressed reverence on the mind of the giddy multitude'.[37] She was taken to the place of execution at Stephen's Green in a cart accompanied by a guard of twenty men from the new Dublin police armed with swords and staves, as well as the sheriffs of Dublin and a party of Lord Drogheda's horse guard. She was strangled and her body was flung into the fire in accordance with the terms of her sentence.[38]

RIOTS ON THE GREEN

During the eighteenth century, the Green was often a meeting place for political gatherings, which sometimes descended into rioting and violence.

One of the earliest recorded riots on St Stephen's Green occurred on 6 June 1700, when rival gangs, the butchers and weavers, squared up to each other to settle a dispute. The gangs initially met on the Green to have a game of football, but they ultimately decided on a forty-a-side battle instead. The fighting was vicious as they went at each other with 'Clubbes, Pikes, Stones, Cleavers and some Guns ...'[39] The weavers eventually got the upper hand and the butchers fled in disarray. The weavers chased them into the butchers' stronghold in Patrick Street, where they gave them another hiding. The butchers' wives tried to help their men by showering the weavers with stones, so the weavers took revenge by pulling some of their houses down.

Six or seven rioters were killed during the incident and

it was reported that several more died from their wounds: 'some having their heads broke, others their arms, backs and leggs in a terrible manner and 'tis thought many of them will die from their wounds'. Around seventy were badly injured in the riot and six of the ringleaders were arrested and taken to Newgate Prison.[40]

A frequent flashpoint was the annual gathering that took place at the Green in June, when Catholics assembled to celebrate the birthday of 'The Pretender', King James. In June 1726 the *Dublin Intelligence* reported that a 'great mob gathered at Stephen's Green'.[41] The Jacobites, wearing white roses, the symbol of King James, had been assembling since early morning, and many were armed with clubs and other weapons. Anyone found wearing a red rose – the symbol of the Protestant opposition – was beaten, as were the constables of the local parish watch, who were sent to the Green to quell the disturbances.

Later on it was reported that the mob were throwing dead cats and dogs around in a bizarre game near Lord Abercorn's house on the Green, when his lordship appeared at a window and ordered them to disperse. In response, someone hit his lordship in the face with a dead cat and the mob smashed all his windows:

> [I]n this city on the Pretender's birthday, in the evening a great mob gathered at Stephen's Green .... they, to begin some game,

fell to toss dead dogs and cats about, which being near the Right Honourable the Lord Abercorn's house, his Lordship, ordering they might disperse, which it seems was not their intention without mischief, for they with abundance of insolence threw one of the dead creatures to the window in order to hit his Lordship in the face and then persisted in their evil intentions with stones and batts with which they broke the windows in a very riotous manner ... [42]

Another man who tried to remonstrate with the rioters from the window of his house in nearby Dawson Street was badly beaten and had his windows broken.

Many of the rioters themselves were injured during the disturbances. Several were reported to be killed or badly injured and fifty or sixty of their number ended up in jails throughout the city.[43] The rioting continued for the rest of the night and there were running battles all over the city.

Away from the rioting that often blighted the Green, however, some very interesting figures are commemorated within its grounds.

MONUMENTS
ON THE GREEN

Over the decades, several memorials and statues of different kinds have been unveiled in the Green. What follows is an account of the main monuments.

FUSILIERS' ARCH

The main entrance to the park at St Stephen's Green is at the top of Grafton Street and is dominated by the granite Fusiliers' Arch. This structure commemorates the soldiers of the Royal Dublin Fusiliers who died fighting in the Boer War in South Africa from 1899 to 1902. The archway, made from Wicklow granite, was unveiled on 19 August 1907 by the Duke of Connaught.

The monument is loosely based on the Arch of Titus in Rome. The design was originally suggested by Sir Thomas Drew and the work was carried out by Howard Pentland of the Royal Hibernian Academy. Money to build the monument was raised by public subscription. The monument also bears the names of the principal engagements in which the regiments took part: Colenso, Hart's Hill, Ladysmith, Laing's Nek, Talana and Tugela Heights.

The archway was not without controversy when it was built, however, and was labelled 'traitors' gate' by nationalists opposed to British rule in Ireland. It didn't help that Irishmen fought on both sides of the conflict in South Africa, and though the vast majority fought on the British side, many Irish people were still in sympathy with the Boers. An Irish brigade led by John MacBride – a future Easter Rising participant – fought on their side against the British. James Connolly was also a staunch supporter of the Boers, as was his fellow signatory to the 1916 Proclamation Tom Clarke. Arthur Griffith, founder of Sinn Féin, also supported the Boers, having lived in South Africa from 1897 to 1899.

Fusilier's Arch at the main entrance to St Stephen's Green.

Despite the criticism, the new monument was generally favourably received by the Dublin press. *The Irish Times* was particularly lavish in its praise:

> *This monument to the gallant deeds of their fellow-countrymen will be for all loyal Irishmen a permanent record of what Ireland has done for the Empire. To the loyal citizens of Dublin especially it will be a continual source of pride and inspiration. We are indeed, 'citizens of no mean city' who can boast of civic brotherhood with those 'bravest of the brave' whose names are written on the Arch in St Stephen's Green.*[44]

But not everyone was as happy. *The Freeman's Journal* was scornful in its attitude to the memorial, saying:

> *From first to last Dublin believed, and believes, the war in which those men were engaged to be unjust and disgraceful. From such a war no glory is to be gained; such a war deserves no commemorating memorial.*[45]

Today, the arch has the distinction of being one of the few colonialist monuments not to have been blown up by Irish republicans in Dublin, although it did sustain some accidental damage during the 1916 Rising. The damage caused by the bullets can still be observed on the monument today.

THE WOLFE TONE MEMORIAL

The Theobald Wolfe Tone memorial, located at the north-west corner of the Green, was erected in 1967. The revolutionary leader is widely regarded as the father of Irish republicanism. Born in Dublin in 1763, Tone was a leading light in the Society of United Irishmen. He died in Dublin on 19 November 1798 after being captured by the British while leading a French military force to Ireland.

The foundation stone for an earlier planned memorial to Tone was actually laid outside the Grafton Street entrance to the Green in 1898, on the anniversary of the 1798 rebellion. It was quarried at Cave Hill in Belfast, where Tone, along with other leaders of the United Irishmen, had pledged his life to free Ireland. It bore the following inscription engraved on a copper plate:

1798
Tribute to Theobald Wolfe
Tone, Patriot.
From the Belfast Nationalist
Centenary Committee

The stone was taken to Dublin from Belfast by train and carried in procession from Parnell Square to Stephen's Green followed by an estimated 100,000 people on 15

The statue of Theobald Wolfe Tone at the north-east corner of St Stephen's Green.

August 1898. The foundation stone also contained a time capsule, with newspapers, coins and a document detailing the history of the Tone family inserted in its centre. The veteran Fenian John O'Leary performed a ceremonial laying of the stone with a silver trowel.

The proposed memorial at the junction of Grafton Street and South King Street never happened, and the stone was eventually removed to City Hall in 1926. During its removal, it was discovered that the papers in the time capsule had been destroyed by water.

New attempts were made to have the memorial erected in 1927, but it was not until 1964 that the current site for the memorial, opposite the Shelbourne Hotel, was made available to the committee.

Following a competition, a design by sculptor Edward Delaney and architect Noel Keating was chosen. The memorial consists of a ten-foot-high bronze figure of Tone backed by a piazza of granite columns and a smaller piazza containing bronze figures. Because of the granite columns, the monument was at one stage known humorously as 'Tonehenge'.

The monument wasn't to everyone's taste. Delaney, sometimes described as Ireland's most controversial sculptor, spoke to the *Irish Independent* about his creation in 1967. He was not too happy with some of the corners cut by the memorial planners in implementing his design. He acknowledged that the committee was acting under financial constraints, but, in a reference to the plaza in front of the statue, he said:

> *It's just a lot of muck ... I asked for a stone entrance and they slapped in concrete ... Don't think I asked for this jumbo jet runway. It's not in proportion with the figure or the granite wall surround.*[46]

Delaney also responded to criticism that his Tone statue was too big, saying that 'Tone figured in a life-size setting would look like a leprechaun ... I was commissioned to make a life-size figure but realised it would look ridiculous, instead of monumental.'

Delaney ended his remarks by answering criticism in relation to the famine figures that also feature in the memorial:

> *Tone's is not a victory monument. He wanted all Ireland independent and united. The failure of Tone's expeditions led to a decline in national morale and presaged the Famine or Great Hunger. If Tone had succeeded I doubt if the Famine would have been allowed to happen.*

The sculptor finished by saying that he would have liked to depict a victorious Tone dressed in a French uniform with a cocked hat and sword, but, he said, 'history decided otherwise'.[47]

The monument was unveiled by President of Ireland Éamon de Valera on 18 November 1967. He lamented the fact that a monument to Tone had not been put in place sooner and noted:

> *It would sorrow Tone's heart not to have the whole nation united, and that there are not here representatives from Belfast of the Presbyterians, those people whom he regarded as the most freedom loving and liberal loving of the whole of our people. Their absence would sorrow him a great deal. But let us have the hope and courage that Wolfe Tone had: let us work to see that his ultimate ideal will be realised.*[48]

Also present at the unveiling was ninety-year-old Kathleen Clarke, a former lord mayor of Dublin and widow of Tom Clarke, one of the signatories of the 1916 Proclamation. The Wolfe Tone Memorial Committee had first been formed in 1898 and no one had done more to keep the committee alive during the intervening years than Kathleen. She had even gone so far as to revive the committee in the late 1950s.

The statue was blown up by the UVF on 8 February 1971. Contemporary reports say that it was blown 20 feet into the air, leaving only the base and the two legs intact. A number of windows at the Shelbourne Hotel and adjoining buildings were shattered in the blast. Delaney was able to restore the damaged statue, however, and it was back in place within a few months of the attack.

As a postscript of sorts, it is interesting to note that a monument to Tone, designed by the English sculptor Francis William Jones, was planned during the 1920s. The memorial committee was split due to the outbreak of the Civil War, however, meaning the project was shelved. Jones's proposed design envisaged a forty-foot-high monument incorporating a twelve-foot-high bronze statue of Tone to be located just outside the main gate of the Green at the top of Grafton Street. That certainly would have seen him tower over the Green in much the same way that he towers over Irish history.

THE STATUE OF GEORGE II

One Stephen's Green statue that you won't see any more is the massive memorial to George II designed by John Van Nost and erected at the centre of the Green in 1758.

On 13 May 1937, the day after the coronation of King George VI, gardaí found three bags of explosives under and around the George II memorial. The area was cordoned off and the bomb squad called. However, the explosives detonated before they reached the Green, resulting in the monument being destroyed.

It was said afterwards that the brass memorial was turned into shells and bullets during 'the Emergency' – elsewhere known as the Second World War – with the remainder of the monument being used for target practice by the Local Defence Force.

ROBERT EMMET

Just inside a small enclave in the railings on the west side of St Stephen's Green, facing the Royal College of Surgeons, stands a statue to Robert Emmet, a United Irishman and leader of the ill-fated rebellion of 1803. Emmet and his small group of revolutionaries had planned a mass uprising against British rule in Ireland, but, during the rebellion, which amounted to little more than a riot in Thomas Street, the small group of republican revolutionaries were captured and the leaders sentenced to death.

Emmet was arrested a month after the attempted rebellion, at a house in Harold's Cross where he had hidden in order to be near his sweetheart, Sarah Curran. During his trial for treason at Green Street courthouse, he made his famous speech from the dock. This included the often quoted lines:

> *Let them and me rest in obscurity and peace; and my tomb*
> *remain uninscribed and my memory in oblivion until other*

The statue of Robert Emmet on the west side of Stephen's Green.

*times and other men can do justice to my character. When my
country takes her place among the nations of the earth, then,
and not till then let my epitaph be written.*[49]

Unfortunately, it still hasn't been possible to write Emmet's
epitaph, because we don't know where he is buried. He
was hanged and beheaded outside St Catherine's church
in Thomas Street on 20 September 1803. Following the
execution, his remains were taken to Kilmainham Gaol,
where it is believed that the artist James Petrie made a
death mask from his severed head. Emmet was initially
buried at Bully's Acre in Kilmainham, but his remains
were removed soon afterwards and taken to an as-yet-
undiscovered location.

Over the years, many theories have been put forward
as to what happened to Emmet's body, but none of these
has proved to be conclusive. At least a dozen sites have
been examined in searches conducted over the last two
centuries, all to no avail.

As for his monument, the seven-foot-high statue by
Jerome Connor was unveiled by Tánaiste Frank Aiken
on 20 January 1968. The statue faces the spot where the
patriot was born at No. 124 St Stephen's Green on 10
March 1778.

Emmet's statue is in fact a replica of a statue, also by
Connor, that was unveiled by President Woodrow Wilson

in Washington in 1917. Another replica was unveiled in Golden Gate Park in San Francisco by Éamon de Valera in 1919.

ANNA AND THOMAS HASLAM

A limestone seat in the centre of Stephen's Green, dedicated to Anna and Thomas Haslam, was carved by the sculptor Albert Power and installed in 1923 in recognition of, as the inscription on the seat reads, 'their long years of public service chiefly devoted to the enfranchisement of women'.

Anna Maria Haslam was born Anna Maria Fisher in Youghal, Co. Cork, in 1829. One of seventeen children, she was the daughter of a miller, Abraham Fisher, and his wife, Jane Moor. The family were Quakers and Anna's parents were committed anti-slavery and peace activists. They were also well known for their charity work, notably during the days of the Great Famine.

Anna was educated at a Quaker school in Waterford and subsequently taught at Ackworth, a Quaker school in Yorkshire. It was there that she met fellow Irishman and teacher Thomas Haslam from Mountmellick, in what was then Queen's County, now Co. Laois.

Thomas, like Anna, was interested in the advancement of rights for women and women's suffrage. Like Anna he was a Quaker, though he had been expelled from the

Society of Friends for an unnamed misdemeanour. This meant that when the couple were married in Cork in 1854, Anna too was expelled from the Quakers.

They lived a celibate marriage, as neither wanted to have children. Thomas appears to have been of the opinion that true manliness could only be expressed by treating women as friends and companions rather than objects of sexual desire.

Thomas and Anna were social reformers and Anna is chiefly remembered today for her work in securing votes for women. The couple went on to found the Irish Women's Suffrage and Local Government Association in 1867. Writing in 1941, the great Irish feminist Hanna Sheehy Skeffington spoke in glowing terms of the contribution made to the cause of feminism by the Haslams:

> *Anna Maria Haslam, a Quaker rebel, one of the old school, the New Woman one, led the movement for Women's Suffrage, ably assisted by her husband Thomas, a libertarian in many fields. The organization founded by them and a few women pioneers (the Women's Suffrage and Local Government Association) did much educative spadework, especially in connection with Local Government.*[50]

One of Anna's greatest achievements was her campaign for the repeal of the Contagious Diseases Act of 1864.

The act allowed for the compulsory medical examination of women suspected of being prostitutes in certain areas near army barracks. It also permitted the internment of women suspected of having venereal disease. Anna strongly opposed the act and was instrumental in having it scrapped in 1886.

Anna was also secretary of the Dublin branch of the Ladies' National Association for the Abolition of the Government Regulation of Vice. Moreover, she was an ardent anti-prostitution campaigner.

Thomas Haslam died in 1917. The following year, the ninety-year-old Anna saw her lifelong ambition of

The limestone bench in St Stephen's Green dedicated to the memory of Anna and Thomas Haslam was carved by the sculptor Albert Power.

securing the vote for women realised when she voted in the parliamentary elections for the very first time.

Anna Haslam died on 28 November 1922.

LOUIE BENNETT

Another person commemorated with a stone seat in the centre of the Green is Louie Bennett. She was born at Garville Avenue in Rathgar in 1870 and educated initially at Alexandra College in Earlsfort Terrace; following this she went on to study music in Germany.

Bennett was interested in women's suffrage and in 1911 formed the Irishwomen's Suffrage Federation with her friend and fellow Rathgar woman Helen Chenevix. The movement was an attempt to bring together a range of disparate suffragist groups in Ireland.

In 1911 the Irish Women Workers' Union (IWWU) was founded with Jim Larkin as its first president. A prominent member, Bennett was active during the 1913 Lockout in Dublin and raised funds for the strikers and their families via appeals in the suffragist newspaper *The Irish Citizen*. She took over the running of the union in 1916, but only on the understanding that there would be no interference from Liberty Hall. Aided by Chenevix and Father John Flanagan, Bennett turned the IWWU into a professional organisation, and within two years she had increased the membership from a few hundred to over 5,000 members.

Before 1916 Bennett, an avowed pacifist, had little interest in the nationalist movement, saying that the issue of women's rights was not compatible with support for nationalism. However, she changed her views following the cold-blooded murder of the well-known pacifist and feminist Francis Sheehy Skeffington by Captain Bowen Colthurst at Rathmines Barracks. During the years that followed, she actively campaigned to publicise the atrocities committed by the Black and Tans in Ireland and was also active in the campaign against conscription during the First World War.

Today, Bennett is chiefly remembered for her role in the laundry workers' strike of 1945, when the IWWU fought and won the right for workers to have a two-week paid holiday every year – a right which was subsequently extended to all Irish workers.

Louie Bennett died on 25 November 1956 at Killiney in Dublin.

***

St Stephen's Green today, with its manicured lawns, exotic trees and walkways, is an oasis of calm in the middle of a busy city and is one of Dublin's best-loved public spaces.

As for the square surrounding the Green, it is one of Dublin's oldest and finest Georgian squares. When originally laid out in the 1660s, it was the largest such square in the world. Since then the wonderful buildings and mansions surrounding it have been the exclusive preserve of the wealthy. The majority of the buildings that we see today were in place by the mid-eighteenth century, and some of the finest of these are to be found on the north side of the Green.

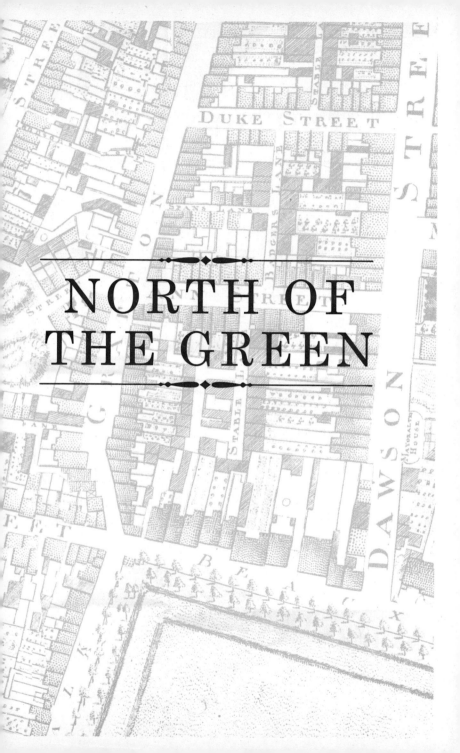

NORTH OF
THE GREEN

NO. 16
ST STEPHEN'S GREEN

No. 16 on the north side of St Stephen's Green, close to the top of Grafton Street, was once the home or palace of several Protestant archbishops of Dublin. The site, now occupied by numbers 16 and 17, was originally a large mansion, the residence of Thomas Wyndham, who served as lord chancellor of Ireland from 1726 to 1739.

The first bishop to inhabit No. 16 was Lord George Beresford, who lived there from 1820 to 1822. He was succeeded by William Magee, a conceited man who liked to parade around the fashionable streets of Dublin on his horse. Magee was a well-known preacher, renowned for his oratorical skills. He was generally known as a tolerant man, but this tolerance did not extend to his Catholic neighbours. He was a staunch opponent of Catholic emancipation and gained notoriety for preventing Wicklow Catholics from worshipping at the cathedral of St Kevin in Glendalough.

Another ecclesiastical resident of No. 16 was Archbishop of Dublin Richard Whately – a known eccentric who was often seen climbing trees in Stephen's Green

No. 16 St Stephen's Green was the home of several archbishops of Dublin.

or playing with his boomerang. He had a fascination for boomerangs and sometimes, during boring meetings, he would make one out of cardboard and fling it around the room to the bemusement of his colleagues. On other occasions he could be seen playing hide and seek with his beloved dogs or throwing stones at crows. He also had his own ideas about medical matters: to cure a headache after he'd been spending too much time at his books, for example, Whately's solution was to go out into the garden with an axe to chop at a tree or a bush until he worked up a sweat, then jump into bed and cover himself with warm blankets until the headache went away.

However, to only focus on Whately's eccentric habits is to do him a disservice. The archbishop was also known as a progressive thinker and an ardent social reformer. Unlike his predecessors, he was a staunch advocate of Catholic emancipation and he also campaigned vigorously to abolish the transportation of Irish prisoners to British colonies throughout the world.

Today he is chiefly remembered for his wit, his sense of humour and his openness, but it has to be said that he was responsible for some of the most dreadful puns ever written down. For example, Whately once posed the question, 'Why can a man never starve in the Great Desert?' The answer was, 'Because he can eat the sand which is [i.e. sandwiches] there.'[1]

Whately was extremely devoted to his wife of forty years, Elizabeth Pope, and when she died in 1863 he was devastated. He became ill soon after her death and resisted all attempts to help him, even to the extent of throwing his medicine out the window. He died that year, aged seventy-seven.

No. 16 certainly had many intriguing characters living in it over the years. It was also originally built by another interesting character – the Dublin developer Gustavus Hume. Hume was a well-known surgeon, referred to as 'Stirabout Gusty' because of his fondness for prescribing porridge to all of his patients.

Today, the ivy-clad building is home to the well-known, upmarket Peploe's restaurant.

THE SHELBOURNE HOTEL

The Shelbourne Hotel dominates the north side of St Stephen's Green and is one of Dublin's, if not the world's, finest hotels.

Founded in 1824 by Martin Burke, the Shelbourne quickly became one of the city's most fashionable establishments. Known initially as Burke's Hotel, it was soon renamed after William, 2nd Earl of Shelburne, who had once lived on the site of the hotel. Following Burke's death in 1863, the hotel was sold to Charles Cotton, Christian Goodman and William Jury. The old building was subsequently demolished and the new Shelbourne Hotel, the one that we know today, opened its doors in 1867.

Over the years, many famous guests have stayed at the Shelbourne. Film stars such as John Wayne, Charlie Chaplin and Elizabeth Taylor have spent time there, as have literary heavyweights and musicians such as Brendan Behan, Luciano Pavarotti and The Rolling Stones.

However, one of the most intriguing figures connected to the hotel must surely be Alois Hitler, half-brother of the German chancellor and Nazi leader Adolf. Alois worked at the Shelbourne as a waiter for a while during the early part of the twentieth century.

At the 1909 Dublin Horse Show in the RDS, where he was posing as a wealthy hotel owner, Alois met Dublin woman Bridget Dowling. The smartly dressed Hitler struck up a conversation with Bridget's father, William, while they were looking at horses. The seventeen-year-old Bridget immediately showed an interest in the handsome young Austrian and they began to meet regularly.

Bridget's family disapproved of the relationship, so the next year she eloped with Alois to London. William Dowling attempted (unsuccessfully) to have Hitler charged with kidnapping. However, father and daughter were reconciled a year later in Liverpool when Bridget gave birth to a son, William Patrick Hitler.

In 1914 Alois abandoned his family and went to Germany to sell razor blades. The First World War kept him there for the next four years. During that time he faked his own death and married again. He was eventually caught and prosecuted for bigamy by the German authorities, but was freed after Bridget spoke up for him in court.

In later years, Bridget and William Patrick attempted to exploit their relationship with the Führer. Bridget's unfinished memoir, entitled *My Brother-in-law Adolf*, was discovered in the New York Public Library in the

1970s, and an edited version of the manuscript was later published by British journalist Michael Unger in 1979.

In the book, Bridget took the credit for introducing Hitler to astrology and claimed to have advised him to trim his moustache. Bridget also revealed in the book – which has largely been written off as a work of fiction – that Adolf Hitler had stayed with her, Alois and baby William at their Liverpool home for a period in 1913.

William Patrick seemed to very much follow in the footsteps of his mother, at one point attempting to blackmail Hitler. He wrote to the Führer, threatening to expose a Jewish connection in their family history. Later on, while working as a car salesman in Germany, he tried to get his uncle to use his influence to get him a better job. Hitler apparently refused his nephew's request, saying that he wouldn't show favouritism towards his family.

William Patrick continued to milk the family connection for all it was worth. In 1937 he said in an interview, 'I am the only legal descendant of the Hitler family.' He then crossed his arms in a gesture that was characteristic of the tyrant and said, 'That gesture must be in the blood. I find myself doing it more and more.'[2]

William went to the US in 1939 with his mother and toured the country giving lectures about his famous uncle. During the Second World War he spent some time in the US Navy. After the war, he changed his name and disappeared from public view. William 'Paddy' Hitler was last seen alive in 1977, somewhere in the New York City metropolitan area. His mother, Bridget Dowling Hitler, was last known to be living at Highgate in London during the 1950s.

One thing is for sure: it has been a long time since a Hitler last set foot inside the Shelbourne, which is still regarded as one of Dublin's premier hotels today. The building underwent a major renovation in 2007 and now boasts 265 bedrooms. It also has thirteen meeting rooms, one of which is the famous Constitution Room, where the Irish constitution was drafted under the chairmanship of Michael Collins in 1922.

KILDARE STREET

Kildare Street, leading from Trinity College to St Stephen's Green, was called Coote Street until around 1756. It was then part of the Molesworth Fields, which took their name from the Molesworth family who owned them. At that time, the Molesworth Fields were an unfashionable wasteland on the periphery of Dublin. According to C. T. McCready in his *Dublin Street Names Dated and Explained*, the street was named after James Fitzgerald, 20th Earl of Kildare and Duke of Leinster.

LEINSTER HOUSE

Today the street is dominated by the magnificent Leinster House. Now home to Dáil Éireann, it was the first mansion to be built in the area. When James Fitzgerald was planning to build Leinster House in the 1740s, he was advised against doing so in such an unfashionable part of the city. However, he ignored the advice, saying, 'they will follow me wherever I go'.[3] How right he was. Leinster House was described by Thomas Malton in 1794 as 'the most stately private edifice in the city'.[4]

Nowadays, Leinster House is the centre building of a group of three elegant structures and is flanked by the National Library of Ireland on one side and the National Museum on the other. The magnificent granite and limestone Palladian mansion was designed by the architect Richard Castle and is still considered one of his greatest achievements.

QUEEN VICTORIA'S STATUE

For forty years between 1908 and 1948 a massive statue commemorating England's Queen Victoria dominated the front of government buildings in Kildare Street.

Famously dubbed 'the auld bitch' by James Joyce, the statue was commissioned by the Royal Dublin Society following the queen's visit to Dublin in April 1900, with the sculptor John Hughes contracted to create it.

The statue consisted of a bronze figure of Victoria, along with secondary Sicilian marble figures representing 'fame', 'peace' and 'plenty'. The statue was unveiled by Lord Aberdeen on 15 February 1908 and it was controversial right from the start. There was a row when it was learned that the pedestal was made in France, but that controversy soon faded away. One commentator referred to it as spectacularly hideous, and the writer and historian Maurice Craig was equally unimpressed with the statue, describing it in the following unflattering terms:

There she sat festooned by seagulls and dripping verdigris on her
white limestone outworks, curiously benevolent in her ugliness,
softening the grim impact of Leinster House.[5]

Following independence in 1922, there were calls for the statue to be removed. Some objected on the grounds that it was ugly, but most of the complainants were understandably unhappy that a giant effigy of the famine queen was sitting on the doorstep of the national parliament. (Victoria was referred to as the 'famine queen' due to the fact that she, and the government she presided over, turned their backs on Ireland during the catastrophe that was the Great Famine.) The calls for the statue's removal intensified in the 1930s, though it wasn't until 1948 that it was removed by the Fine Gael government of the time and replaced by a car park.

The bronze statue of Victoria was initially moved to the Royal Hospital in Kilmainham, followed by a stint at a former industrial school in Daingean, Co. Offaly. The statue eventually found a permanent home at a shopping centre in Sydney, Australia.

THE ROYAL COLLEGE OF PHYSICIANS

This beautiful building, with its handsome portico of Portland stone at No. 6 Kildare Street, is the headquarters of the Royal College of Physicians, the oldest medical corporation in Ireland. It was established in the seventeenth century as the Fraternity of Physicians and its first headquarters was on College Green, or Hoggen Green as it was then called, beside Trinity College.

The college was initially part of Trinity College, but the two institutions fell out and the physicians went out on their own for a period. Harmony was restored in 1711, however, when Trinity opened its own medical school, and both bodies worked closely with each other thereafter.

The physicians moved into the building at No. 6, which was once occupied by the Kildare Street Club, in 1867 and have been there ever since. The Royal College of Physicians was the first medical institution in Ireland or Britain to register women as medical practitioners, and many British women doctors were enabled to practise their trade by gaining their qualifications through this institution.

NAPOLEON'S TOOTHBRUSH

One curious artefact on display at the Royal College of Physicians is Napoleon Bonaparte's toothbrush, along with a few other items that once belonged to the 'Little Corporal'.

The items were given to Dublin-born Barry Edward O'Meara, who was the surgeon on the British naval ship *Bellerophon* with Napoleon after the Frenchman had surrendered at the Battle of Waterloo in 1815. When he was exiled to the island of St Helena, Napoleon asked the British to allow O'Meara to travel to St Helena with him as his personal physician. His request was granted, although O'Meara only agreed on the basis that he would act solely as Napoleon's physician and not as a spy. The two men became firm friends during their stay on the island.

Napoleon urged O'Meara to keep a diary during his stay on St Helena, telling him that it would make him a fortune after the Frenchman's death. In recognition of O'Meara's service and friendship, Napoleon gave him several gifts, which included two snuff boxes and the toothbrush now on display in Kildare Street.

O'Meara was expelled from the island in June 1818 when the governor of St Helena, Sir Hudson Lowe, decided that he was getting too close to Napoleon. On his return to London, O'Meara demanded better treatment for Napoleon from the British Admiralty and told them that their captive was in fact dying. The Admiralty Board asked O'Meara to keep quiet about Napoleon's health and offered him a lucrative post at the Chelsea and Greenwich naval hospital as a sweetener. O'Meara refused to have any part of it and was dismissed from the navy without a pension. He also lost his licence to practise medicine.

Undaunted by this setback, O'Meara set himself up as a dentist on the Edgeware Road in London and hung

Napoleon's wisdom tooth in the front window. Napoleon died in 1821 and a year later O'Meara published his diary, *Napoleon in Exile, or a Voice from St. Helena.* The book was a huge success and made O'Meara a wealthy man.

O'Meara was a staunch supporter of Daniel 'the Liberator' O'Connell, who led the successful campaign for Catholic emancipation during the 1820s. It was said that O'Meara died after catching a chill at one of O'Connell's rallies. He died in London on 12 July 1836 at the age of fifty-three. After his death, O'Meara's collection of Napoleon memorabilia passed through several hands before it was eventually donated to the Royal College of Physicians in 1936.

KILDARE STREET CLUB

The Kildare Street Club began life in 1782 when William Burton Conyngham was barred from the infamous Daly's Club on College Green. In response to his banishment, Conyngham set up his own club with some friends at No. 6 Kildare Street, though the members later decided to build a bigger and better club during the 1850s on the corner of Kildare Street and Nassau Street. Both Kildare Street and Daly's were gentlemen's drinking and gaming clubs.

Trouble often surrounded these clubs, and Kildare Street was no exception. The club was the focal point for rioters in 1861, when they smashed all the windows in protest at Prince Albert's visit to Dublin.

Writing in 1886, George Moore, in his book *Parnell and his Island*, said that the Kildare Street Club:

> *is one of the most important institutions in Dublin ... This club is a sort of oyster bed into which all the eldest sons of the landed gentry fall as a matter of course. There they remain spending their days drinking sherry and cursing Gladstone in a sort of dialect, a dead language which the larva-like stupidity of the club has preserved.*[6]

The Kildare Street Club continued in existence until 1976, when it merged with the Dublin University Club on St Stephen's Green.

THE FIRST HORSE SHOW

The Dublin Horse Show at the RDS is an annual feature in Dublin's sporting and social calendar and regularly attracts over 100,000 visitors during the week-long event. However, the very first horse show staged by the Royal Dublin Society took place on Leinster Lawn, in the grounds of Leinster House.

Horse shows had taken place previously, but these events – run by the Royal Agricultural Society – were effectively sideshows at their annual agricultural fair. The first of these, organised by Lord Howth, took place on Leinster Lawn on 15 April 1864. The second took place in September 1866.

In 1867 the Agricultural Society and the Royal Dublin Society – alarmed at the declining number of horses in Ireland – decided to hold a show exclusively for horses and this took place in Stephen's Green during the month of September. This experiment proved so successful that the Royal Dublin Society decided to make it an annual event, one that has endured to the present day.

The first horse show run exclusively for horses by the Royal Dublin Society was held over three days, beginning on 28 July 1868 at Leinster House. Despite poor attendance on the opening day – mainly due to bad weather and the exorbitant admission price of ten shillings – matters improved greatly over the following two days. The entrance fee was hastily reduced to five shillings, and then to two shillings and sixpence, which had the desired effect of increasing the number of visitors.

Nearly 400 horses took part in the show and there were over 6,000 visitors, who were entertained by military bands and a wide variety of sideshows. There was also a wide range of commercial stands in evidence at the first show, many of which were household names in the city. Dockrell's of South Great George's Street display, for example, contained a wide array of kitchenware, bathroom and plumbing goods, as well as an extensive selection of wall coverings, glassware and chimney frames. Meanwhile, Kennan's of Fishamble Street displayed their new and improved lawnmowing machines, as well as a new invention for levelling gravel called a 'gravel scuffler' and a wide range of garden tools and furnishings.

One of the main attractions of the show was the jumping event that took place in the courtyard of Leinster House on the first day of the show. The event had only been added to the programme three days earlier on the suggestion of Lord Howth, who urged the committee to organise a jumping competition along the same lines as the Islington horse show. However, so many people gathered to view the jumping competition that the makeshift wooden terraces collapsed, throwing many spectators into the mud. There were no reports of any injuries and the showjumping event was won by a horse called 'Shane Rua' owned by a Mr R. Flynn.

In 1881 the Dublin Horse Show moved to its present location at Ballsbridge. At the time that the move was being proposed, it was feared in many quarters that Dubliners would not travel to what was then seen as the outskirts of the city for the event. However, these fears proved groundless and the show continued to grow until it became the international event that it is today.

***

Today, Kildare Street is chiefly known as the home of Irish politics and politicians. Leinster House is the place where Dáil Éireann (the Irish Assembly) and Seanad Éireann (the Senate) have sat since 1922. The street is also home to two of Ireland's most important cultural institutions in the National Library of Ireland and the National Museum. The National Library preserves and protects the documentary and intellectual record of Ireland, while the National Museum houses some of the state's greatest archaeological and cultural treasures, such as the Ardagh Chalice, the Tara Brooch and the Derrynaflan Hoard. Both the library and museum are visited by thousands annually.

DAWSON STREET

Dawson Street, home of the lord mayor of Dublin and haunt of sophisticated diners, has been one of Dublin city's most fashionable thoroughfares for over 350 years. The street was first named in 1705 after Joshua Dawson, one of the secretaries of state for Ireland, who bought a narrow strip of land between Grafton Street and the Molesworth Fields leading from St Patrick's Well Lane (now Nassau Street) to Stephen's Green. Up to that time, the Molesworth Fields and surrounding lands were considered to be out in the countryside. Dawson bought the land from Henry Temple, Earl of East Sheen in Surrey, and a Dublin merchant named Hugh Price, in 1705, and during the following years he developed it into one of the city's finest streets.

THE MANSION HOUSE

Joshua Dawson's house was bought by the City of Dublin in 1715 to be used as a residence for the lord mayor. John Gilbert's *History of the City of Dublin* records that it cost £3,500. That included the house and its contents free of all rent except 'one loaf of double refined sugar, of six pounds weight' to be paid to the representatives of Dawson each Christmas.

Dawson also agreed to construct a room 33 feet long and 14 feet wide for the lord mayor, which would include goods and furniture itemised thus:

> *Twenty-four brass locks; six marble chimney pieces; the tapestry hangings; silk window curtains and window seats, and chimney glass in the great bed-chambers; the gilt leather hangings; four pairs of scarlet calamanco window curtains; and chimney glass in the Dantzick oak parlour; the Indian calico window-curtains and seats, and chimney-glass in the Dantzick oak parlour; the window curtains and chimney-glass in the large eating room.[7]*

No expense was spared in the particulars for the home of the city's first citizen and so, since 1715, the Mansion House has been Dublin's centre of hospitality for visiting dignitaries.

LORD MAYOR'S COACH

In recent years Dublin's mayors have been reasonably well looked after in transport terms, certainly compared to their counterparts of 300 years ago. Most of today's mayors are provided with a set of wheels and a driver to ferry them around the city so they can carry out their duties.

However, up until 1791, Dublin Corporation had no state coach and the lord mayor had to provide his own transport or else walk to civic functions. For instance, can you imagine the embarrassment of the lord mayor in 1701 when he was forced to walk behind the carriages of the lords justices to the unveiling of a statue to King William of Orange on College Green?

Things were slightly better for Lord Mayor Humphrey French in 1732, who made what *Pue's Occurrences* described as 'the greatest appearance that was ever known on such an occasion' at King George II's birthday bash at Dublin Castle in October of that year. French's coach was reportedly pulled by six horses and manned by several elaborately dressed footmen.

Nearly twenty years later, however, the lord mayor was back on foot again. Newspapers reported in July 1751 that the mayor of the time, John Cooke, walked from the Tholsel in High Street to lay the foundation stone of the new Rotunda Hospital in Great Britain Street (now Parnell Street).

The City Assembly did toy with the idea of buying a coach in 1763, but nothing further was done about it. Three years later the problem was solved by the Duke of Leinster, who donated a 'Berlin' coach to the city of Dublin. This coach was used for twenty years until it became too costly to keep it in a decent state of repair.

In 1789 the corporation finally decided that a new coach should be built, and William Whitton, a Dominick Street coach-builder, won the contract. There were at least thirty coach-building firms in the city at that time, mostly based on the northside.

Whitton began the building of the coach using the best artists and craftsmen available to him, and it was ready for use by November 1790. However, just before the coach was due to be displayed to the public, Lord Clare's London-built coach, costing £7,000, appeared on the streets of Dublin. The corporation was determined to show that anything London could do they could do better, so they decided to ask Whitton to redesign the state coach. The new and improved Dublin coach appeared on the streets one year later, just in time for the celebration of William of Orange's birthday on 4 November.

Unlike ninety years earlier, this time the lord mayor didn't have to walk to the party. King Billy would have been pleased, too, as on each corner of the roof of the coach was a carved figure of a child carrying bunches of orange lilies. The Dublin coach cost a total of £2,690 to build, less than half the cost of its London rival.

During the twentieth century, the state coach was only used sporadically. It made a rare appearance at the Eucharistic Congress in 1932. The coach reappeared in 1976 after it was completely restored by Dublin Corporation.

It has remained an annual feature of Dublin's St Patrick's Day parade ever since.

MORRISON'S HOTEL AND ST PATRICK'S WELL

During the nineteenth century, Morrison's Hotel, also known as the Leinster Hotel and Tavern, on the corner of Dawson Street and Nassau Street, was one of the city's largest and most expensive hotels.

The hotel has many historical connections and many historical figures stayed there. Charles Dickens stayed at Morrison's when he was in town, for example, as did the infamous Captain William Bligh – the commanding officer on board the *Bounty*, of *Mutiny on the Bounty* fame.

The 'uncrowned king of Ireland' and leader of the Land League, Charles Stewart Parnell, was also a regular guest at Morrison's. He was actually arrested at the hotel on 13 October 1881 by two detectives from the G Division of the Dublin Metropolitan Police. Accused of inciting un-named persons to withhold rents due to landlords, he re-fused to leave until he got a discount off his hotel bill. He was then taken to Kilmainham, where he was incarcerated under the Coercion Act until May of the following year. (The Coercion Act of 1881 effectively allowed people to be imprisoned without trial.)

Morrison's was just over the road from the famous St Patrick's Well. It was said that water from the well was used in the hotel. The ancient spring was one of hundreds throughout Ireland associated with St Patrick and, according to legend, the saint had prayed for a spring to appear in that spot as he felt sorry for the citizens of Dublin and their lack of fresh drinking water. The well attracted thousands of pilgrims in its day and was believed to have healing properties. Some described the water from the spring as being very hot, while others described it as being exceptionally pure.

Every year, on 17 March, St Patrick's Day, huge crowds gathered at this well to drink and wash themselves in the water. By all accounts, water wasn't the only beverage being consumed at the well, and there are numerous tales of pilgrims indulging in riotous behaviour in its vicinity for days afterwards.

The well dried up in 1729, but it was cleaned out and unblocked two years later after complaints from the public. As the years progressed, however, the water supply to the well dwindled and it eventually dried up once again.

St Patrick's Well wasn't the only spring in the area; there were several behind Nassau Street and Kildare Street. There was even a well found under the lawn at Leinster House in 1860.

Around that time, a man named Edward Clibborn set out to see if he could discover the exact site of the famous well and he found that there were in fact several in that immediate area – all of which were claimed as St Patrick's original well. After a thorough examination of the available evidence, Clibborn came to the conclusion that the most likely contender to the title was a well behind No. 9 Nassau Street. Clibborn says that during the mid-eighteenth century this well was accessed by a flight of steps from the nearby Frederick Lane.

Interest in St Patrick's Well, like the spring itself, dried up until the soft drinks and mineral water company, Cantrell & Cochrane, bought a premises in Nassau Place and harvested the spring waters from several wells in the area previously known as the Molesworth Fields. The springs were known to be of the highest quality and Cantrell & Cochrane were not slow to exploit the legend of St Patrick's Well in marketing its products. The company employed hundreds of workers at its factory and its beverages were exported to Britain and further afield to the USA, Australia and India.

Today, nearly all of the wells have either dried up or been covered over. One well still remains just inside the Nassau Street entrance to Trinity College, but it is not accessible to the public.

FELICIA HEMANS

One famous resident of Dawson Street was the English poet Felicia Hemans, who lived at No. 21. She was born in Liverpool in 1793 and was the daughter of merchant George Browne and Austrian woman Felicity Wagner.

No. 21 Dawson Street.

Hemans is best known for her poem 'Casabianca', which is usually remembered these days as 'the boy stood on the burning deck'. It was published in 1826 and is about an incident that occurred on board the French ship *Orient* during the Battle of the Nile in 1798, when the captain's young son Giaconte refused to abandon his post and was killed in an explosion on board the ship.

The boy stood on the burning deck
Whence all but he had fled;
The flame that lit the battle's wreck
Shone round him o'er the dead[8]

The poem was popular in Britain up until the 1950s and has been mentioned in literature, drama and numerous

TV programmes and movies down through the years, as well as being parodied relentlessly.

Bram Stoker name-checked the poem in *Dracula* and it appeared in P. G. Wodehouse's *The Luck of the Bodkins*. C. S. Forester used the title 'the boy stood on the burning deck' for a short story about the Battle of Midway.

Felicia came to Dublin in 1831 to be with her brother, Colonel George Browne, who was head of the Dublin Metropolitan Police (DMP) at that time, and lived at Upper Pembroke Street and Stephen's Green before moving to Dawson Street. However, Colonel Browne was forced to resign his post in controversial circumstances in 1858.

In those days, the arrival of a new lord lieutenant in Dublin was traditionally marked by a state procession through the streets of the city, and when Archibald William Montgomerie, 13th Earl of Eglinton, was appointed to that position in early 1858, the municipal authorities made the usual arrangements for his arrival.

Montgomerie arrived at Westland Row railway station on 3 March of that year, where he was greeted by the lord mayor and corporation of Dublin. He was escorted with great pomp and ceremony through the streets on his way to Dublin Castle.

At College Green, where the majority of the crowd had gathered to witness the spectacle, a large group of students from Trinity College assembled just inside the railings. They were heavily armed with a variety of missiles, including stones, eggs, oranges and firecrackers. Although the lord lieutenant was allowed to pass through College Green unmolested, the students indiscriminately pelted everyone else in sight with their missiles. There was no particular motive for the unrest in College Green that day and the students – not for the first time – appeared to be indulging purely in a spot of recreational rioting.

There was a large detachment of the DMP on duty that day outside the college and they soon became the object of the students' attention. They threw firecrackers and gravel at the police horses and several policemen had their helmets knocked off during the melee. The junior dean of the college, Dr Stubbs, pleaded with the students to withdraw, but his words fell on deaf ears.

Colonel George Browne was in charge of police operations at College Green that day. He was hit in the eye by a missile and, enraged, ordered his men to attack the students. The DMP, some on horseback, drew their batons and sabres and charged through the gates of the college, trampling the students and using their batons at will. The students eventually managed to flee to safety inside the college walls, but not before at least thirty of their number were injured. Many received wounds of a serious nature, and one student named William Leeson was carried in an unconscious state from the scene. It wasn't all one-way traffic, though, as eighteen policemen were also injured.

The riot received a great deal of attention in the press and 4,000 people signed a petition in the tobacco shop opposite Trinity demanding an inquiry into the behaviour of the police. Questions were asked in relation to the incident in the British House of Lords and the House of Commons, ultimately resulting in the British government launching an inquiry into the events. It has to be said that, in normal circumstances, beating young men off the street would not have been a problem for the Dublin police, but the young men injured in the riot that day were the sons of some of the most influential people in Ireland.

Colonel Browne eventually admitted full responsibility for the incident, and he, along with seven of his colleagues, were sent forward for trial at Green Street courthouse on 21 June 1858.

Dr John Stubbs gave evidence that he had allowed the students to watch the procession on the strict understanding that they behave themselves, and he stated that he had confiscated a basket of eggs from one student and sticks from another. William Leeson, who had been carried from the scene in an unconscious state, claimed that he was unarmed and had taken no part in the riot and was simply heading towards the gates when he was attacked.

The DMP gave evidence that they had been severely

provoked by the students, with one constable claiming that he was forced to draw his sword when a student attempted to cut the reins of his horse. Another constable stated that while the DMP on horseback had indeed drawn their swords, the students were only hit with the flat side to avoid doing them too much damage.

The jury retired to consider the evidence and returned just five minutes later with a verdict of not guilty for Colonel Browne. However, he still resigned from his post as commissioner of police shortly afterwards.

As for Felicia Hemans, she died at her home in 1835 at the age of forty-one after contracting scarlet fever. Some believed at the time that she had become ill after sitting too long in the gardens at the Royal Dublin Society, which were then in the grounds of Leinster House in Kildare Street. She is buried in a vault just across the road from her home, in St Ann's church in Dawson Street, and a stained-glass window in her honour was installed in the church in 1860.

**

Today, Dawson Street is one of Dublin's most fashionable thoroughfares, boasting many fine examples of Georgian architecture, including one of the city's finest libraries, the Royal Irish Academy, as well as Dublin's oldest bookshop, Hodges Figgis.

Over the centuries the street has become a thriving commercial hub, hosting restaurants, cafés and a wide variety of other businesses. When Joshua Dawson was planning the street over 300 years ago, he stipulated that no shops, pubs or commercial activity of any kind were to be allowed on the street, so he might not be too happy if he could see his creation today.

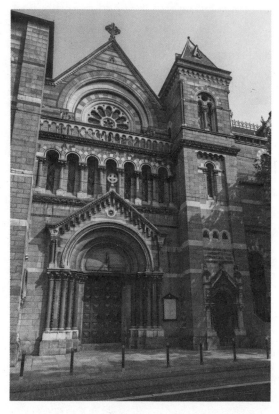

St Ann's church, Dawson Street.

GRAFTON
STREET

Grafton Street is Dublin's premier shopping district and is currently one of the world's most expensive places to rent retail property. The street was laid out at the end of the seventeenth century and was originally known as 'the highway' to St Stephen's Green, leading from All Hallows (Trinity College) to the Green. The street was only partially laid out at this time and the southern end was a wheat field known as 'Crosses Garden'. Grafton Street was named after Henry Fitzroy, the 1st Duke of Grafton.

From its earliest times, Grafton Street was a fashionable residential street and home to many well-known personalities. The manager of Dublin's famous Smock Alley Theatre was a resident, as was the family of Charles Robert Maturin, the Gothic novelist.

The street underwent further development in 1712 when Dublin Corporation designated it a 'crown causeway'. When Carlisle Bridge (now O'Connell Bridge) was built in 1792, Grafton Street became more commercialised and many of the residential buildings were converted into shops. There were also a number of taverns on the street, as well as lottery offices, bookshops and private schools.

CAFÉ CAIRO AND BEWLEYS

The Café Cairo at No. 59 Grafton Street – the site currently occupied by United Colors of Benetton – was rumoured to have sometimes been used as a meeting place by British spies and informers during the War of Independence in Ireland from 1919 to 1921. It is possible that the infamous Cairo Gang (a notorious group of British spies who were sent to Ireland during the War of Independence) gained its name from the café.

Whether that was true or not, the Café Cairo was certainly a meeting place for Dublin's literati and political types. Kevin O'Shiel, a barrister, journalist and politician, painted a fascinating picture of some of the goings on at the café during that period. According to O'Shiel, some of Ireland's leading literary figures would gather daily at the café to discuss literature and the events of the day. The regular clientele at these gatherings included Ernest A. Boyd, one of Ireland's finest literary critics, and the artists Ferdinand Tuohy and Leo Whelan. O'Shiel tells an amusing tale concerning Boyd and the Irish writer and parliamentarian Darrell Figgis. Figgis met Boyd one day in The Bailey in Duke Street and, according to O'Shiel, Boyd was 'in a state of exasperated and frustrated amusement'.[9]

The reason for his merriment was that Tuohy had been hired by the nuns in North Great George's Street to paint a picture of Jesus for them, and he had made Boyd sit for it. Figgis laughed at the notion of Boyd posing as Christ and said, 'Just fancy, the holy nuns will henceforth be praying to that atheist Boyd.'[10]

O'Shiel said that Boyd and Figgis often clashed and vied with each other for the limelight, and that 'they both kept beards; and in those universally clean-shaven times one rarely saw two bearded men as friends'.[11] Figgis would later lose his beard, at least temporarily, in 1922, when a group of anti-Treaty IRA men broke into his house in Rathmines and shaved it off in retaliation for his making derogatory comments about them in the press.

Other well-known figures in Dublin at that time, such as the writer James Stephens, academic Mario Esposito, journalist and author Frank Gallagher, and Charles Bewley, who was Ireland's envoy to Germany from 1933 to 1939, were also regulars at the Café Cairo. Bewley – whose family owned the famous Bewley's café just down the road – was an unashamed supporter of the Nazis and a confirmed anti-Semite.

The first indications that Bewley held anti-Semitic beliefs came in 1921, when Michael Collins sent him to Berlin along with IRA quartermaster Robert Briscoe, who would later become lord mayor of Dublin, to buy arms.

Bewley and Briscoe went for a drink in a Jewish music hall in Berlin, but Bewley was thrown out after making anti-Semitic comments.

From 1929 until 1933 Bewley worked for the Irish foreign service at the Vatican in Rome. He was appointed minister to Germany in August 1933, just after the Nazis had seized power. He was dismissed from his post on the eve of the Second World War, and was then given a job writing Nazi propaganda for a Swedish news agency by Joseph Goebbels.

Suspected of being a Nazi collaborator, Bewley was arrested in Austria after the Second World War had ended. He was interned by the Allies from May 1945 until December of that year. It seemed for a time that Bewley might be hanged, but he was eventually released following intervention by the Irish authorities.

On his release, Bewley went to live in Rome, where he spent the remainder of his days writing and drinking coffee. In 1956 his highly sympathetic biography of Hermann Göring, *Hermann Göring and the Third Reich*, was published. Bewley died in Rome in 1969 and his memoirs, entitled *Memoirs of a Wild Goose*, were published in 1989.

The Bewley family, best known for its cafés around Dublin city, were Quakers. The family business was founded by Joshua Bewley, who was a tea merchant in the 1840s, and had its headquarters at Sycamore Alley. Joshua senior ran the business with his sons, Joshua and Ernest, and when Joshua junior emigrated to Australia in the 1890s, Ernest was left in charge of the business. Following a family row, Ernest expanded into the coffee

Ernest Bewley opened the café on the site of Samuel Whyte's Academy in 1927.

business and opened cafés at South Great George's Street, Westmoreland Street, Fleet Street and, in 1927, Grafton Street. Today, the Grafton Street café is the only one that remains open. It closed for refurbishment in 2015, but reopened on 1 November 2017 after a multi-million renovation programme.

SAMUEL WHYTE'S ACADEMY

Samuel Whyte's Academy, or the 'Seminary for the Instruction of Youth', once stood on the site where Bewley's is now. This academy catered for the education of some of Dublin's wealthiest families. Whyte himself had been educated at Samuel Edwards' Academy in Golden Lane, which is a five-minute walk from Grafton Street. When his father died in 1757, Whyte used his inheritance to set up his own school.

Whyte's first cousin, the novelist and dramatist Frances Chamberlain, was related through marriage to Thomas Sheridan, the manager of Dublin's Smock Alley Theatre. It was through her influence that Whyte managed to attract the children of the city's great and good to his academy.

Whyte had the reputation of being the best teacher in the city and, unusually for that time, he took on boys and girls, both Catholic and Protestant, and taught them a wide range of subjects, including English literature, maths, history and astronomy, among others. When it came to equal opportunities for men and women, Whyte was way ahead of his time. He encouraged and promoted male and female actors at the academy, and one of his publications included an essay entitled 'Respecting Young Ladies as well as Gentlemen'.

Today, the plaque on the wall outside Bewley's mentions some of Whyte's most famous pupils, such as the playwright Richard Brinsley Sheridan; his sister, the writer Alicia Sheridan Le Fanu; the poet Thomas Moore; Robert Emmet; and the Duke of Wellington, Arthur Wellesley.

Thomas Moore often spoke in glowing terms about the education he had received at Whyte's Academy and was full of praise for his former master. When he was just fourteen, Moore wrote a poem to Samuel Whyte, and he later described his school as the best in Dublin:

> As soon as I was old enough to encounter the crowd of a large school, it was determined that I should go to the best then in Dublin, – the grammar school of the well-known Samuel Whyte, whom a reputation of more than thirty years standing had placed at that time at the head of his profession. The talent for recitation and acting which I had so early manifested was the talent of all others which my new schoolmaster was most inclined to encourage; and it was not long before I

attained the honour of being singled out by him on days of public examination, as one of his most successful and popular exhibitors, to the no small jealousy, as may be supposed, of all other mammas, and the great glory of my own. As I looked particularly infantine for my age, the wonder was, of course, still more wonderful.[12]

One of Whyte's most famous pupils was the patriot Robert Emmet, who studied oratory and fencing at the academy.

Whyte himself was said to have been a dab hand with the cane as opposed to the foil. William Fitzpatrick, in his *Lady Morgan: Her Career, Literary and Personal*, describes Whyte as a severe disciplinarian:

Mr, Q_____, now in his eighty-first year, is, with one exception, the last surviving pupil of Whyte's. That gentleman is our authority for the statement that the late Duke of Wellington received instructions at Whyte's academy. Mr. Q_____ has heard his old preceptor vauntingly declare that he had flogged the breech of the subjugator of Tippoo Saib. How vastly would Mr. Whyte's pride have increased, had he lived to boast that the conqueror of Napoleon had been under his hand; and piteously cried for mercy at his knees! Mr. Q_____ tells us that Whyte's taste and talent for flogging were not inferior to Mr. Squeers's passion in the same direction. Although his right

*arm was short almost to deformity, it possessed great strength,
and was the terror of every pupil. 'Such brutal flogging,'
observes Mr. Q_____, 'would now no more be tolerated
than an insolent attempt at assault and battery on the public
streets.'[13]*

Following the Act of Union of 1800, the academy
suffered a downturn and numbers declined drastically.
Whyte retired and died at his home in Grafton Street in
September 1811. He was buried at St Ann's church on
Dawson Street.

SAMUEL LOVER

Samuel Lover was born at 60 Grafton Street on 24 February 1797, the son of a wealthy stockbroker. This was
a turbulent time in Irish
history. Lover was fifteen
months old when the 1798
rebellion broke out and
Robert Emmet's attempted
rising in 1803 made a deep
impression on him.

Lover also retained a
vivid memory of the day that
a soldier and a drummer boy
came to his home looking

*No. 60 Grafton Street, the home
of the writer Samuel Lover.*

for a place to sleep. During that unsettled period, it was normal practice for soldiers to be billeted on the people of Dublin whether they liked it or not, but wealthier types – such as the Lovers – had the option of paying them a shilling instead of a bed for the night.

Mrs Lover offered the pair two shillings to go away, but the soldier refused and forced his way into the house, pushing the frightened woman out onto the steps. When Mr Lover returned some time later to find his wife locked out of her own home, he was outraged and went into the house to confront the soldier. The soldier attacked the stockbroker with a bayonet, but Lover senior managed to overpower him until a senior officer arrived on the scene to take the soldier away.

As a child, Lover was educated at the nearby Samuel Whyte's Academy. Lover's father wanted his son to follow him into the family business, but young Samuel had other ideas. He had a flair for music and art and so, much against his father's wishes, he left home to make his way as an artist.

By the time of his twentieth birthday Lover had acqui-red a reputation as a miniature portrait painter of merit and was much in demand among the gentry of Dublin who wished to have their portraits painted. He became a member of the Royal Hibernian Academy (RHA) and in 1830 was made secretary of that organisation. One of his best-known works was his portrait of the violinist Niccolò Paganini, which was exhibited in the RHA in 1833. Lover was also a talented political caricature artist and many of his designs appeared in a popular publication known as *The Irish Horn Book*.

Lover died on 6 July 1868 in London, quite far from Grafton Street, and is buried alongside his two daughters at Kensal Green cemetery.

***

Grafton Street may have started out as a narrow track or laneway leading from College Green to St Stephen's Green, but the street today bears little or no resemblance to its humble origins. It was widened and improved by the Wide Streets Commissioners during the 1840s, with many of the shops, buildings and façades that we see on the street today added at that time. Completely pedestrianised during the 1980s, Grafton Street today is still the most fashionable street in Dublin. It hosts an eclectic mix of buskers, mime artists and flower sellers, which prove a major attraction for locals and visitors alike.

BALFE STREET

Balfe Street is a small laneway just to the west of Grafton Street and is chiefly known today as the home of the upmarket Westbury Hotel. The street was named after the famous composer Michael Balfe in 1917, but up to that point it had been known as Pitt Street, after the former prime minister of Great Britain, William Pitt.

Michael Balfe was born at No. 10 Pitt Street, but he was by no means its most famous (or infamous) resident. That honour goes to Dublin's best-known courtesan, Peg Plunkett, who ran the city's top bordello in Pitt Street during the latter part of the eighteenth century.

PEG PLUNKETT/MARGARET LEESON

The first edition of the memoirs of the notorious Dublin madam Peg Plunkett was published under the title *Memoirs of Mrs Margaret Leeson* in 1795. Not for a very long time had the publication of any biography caused such consternation and panic amongst the ranks of Dublin's ruling classes. The celebrated Peg, also known as Margaret Leeson, was born into a wealthy Westmeath family in 1727 and her clients included a bishop, two lord lieutenants, a governor of the Bank of Ireland and the infamous 'Sham Squire', Francis Higgins.

Peg's first venture was a brothel in Drogheda (now O'Connell) Street, which she ran in partnership with another famous madam, Sally Hayes. For a time, the madams, as Peg tells us, 'lived in an endless round of pleasures' at Drogheda Street.[14] They had a box at the theatre and frequently travelled to the races at the Curragh in their coach.

Their idyllic existence came to an end when they were forced to leave Drogheda Street after a 'brat-pack' known as the 'Pinkindindies', led by the balloonist Richard Crosbie, wrecked the brothel during a riot. Peg had Crosbie – whom she referred to in her memoirs as 'Mr. Balloon' – arrested and prosecuted for the attack on her house. In her memoirs, she said that she had been eight months pregnant at the time of the attack and had lost her baby as a consequence. Crosbie threatened to kill her and he was sent to Newgate Prison for a spell. He was eventually released after Wolfe Tone interceded with Peg on his behalf, telling her that the authorities 'would surely hang him' if she proceeded with the case.[15]

Peg then moved to a premises on Wood Street; one of her regular visitors there was the Bank of Ireland governor David La Touche (1729–1817), who, according to Peg, spent most of his time admiring himself in her large looking glass.

In 1784 Peg opened a new high-class brothel in Pitt Street, on the site where the Westbury Hotel now stands. This establishment, which was sometimes known as 'the Pitt Street Nunnery', was staffed by liveried servants, footmen and a coach driver. In Peg's own words, they were 'a fresh importation of delicious Filles-de-Joies', recruited from the brothels of Covent Garden and Drury Lane in London.

One of the first visitors to the new establishment was Charles Manners, Duke of Rutland and lord lieutenant of Ireland, who, to the amusement of the citizens gathered outside, emerged from the brothel after a period of sixteen hours. His troop of horse guards were not so amused, however, as they had had to wait outside for him throughout the cold November night.

The duke obviously enjoyed his stay at Peg's as he arranged for her to receive a pension of £300 per year under an assumed name.

Peg was married for a very brief period to Barry Yelverton Junior, the profligate son of the Chief Baron of the Irish Exchequer. The Chief Baron gladly handed over 500 guineas to Peg to have the marriage annulled.

Peg's career took a sudden downturn in 1794, when she ran out of money and was arrested and locked up in a debtors' prison. She was released following the intervention of her friends, who combined to pay her debts. She wrote her memoirs soon afterwards to raise some money.

Peg suffered a devastating misfortune when she was raped by five men on her way home from a friend's house in Drumcondra. She contracted a venereal disease during the attack and died at a friend's house in Fownes Street just three months later, in March 1797. She was buried at St James's churchyard in James's Street and her obituary was carried in the *Dublin Evening Post* and the London-based *Gentleman's Magazine*.

There's no trace remaining of Peg's high-class establishment today, with Balfe Street now dominated by the Westbury.

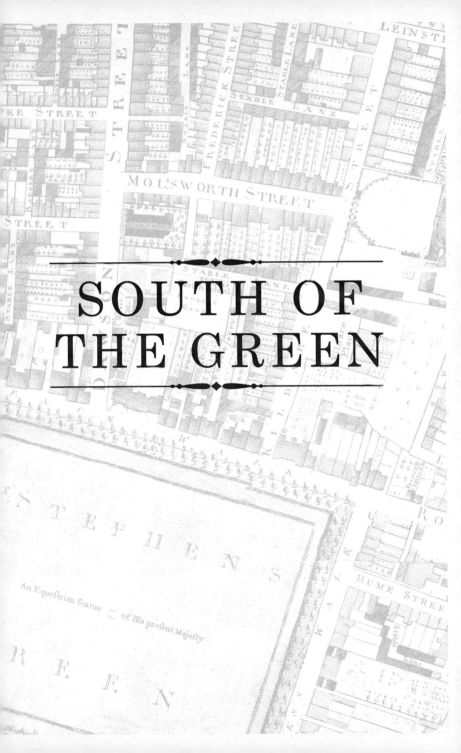

SOUTH OF
THE GREEN

ST STEPHEN'S GREEN SOUTH

Some famous and notorious figures have lived on the south side of St Stephen's Green over the centuries.

BUCK WHALEY

No. 86 on Stephen's Green south, next door to University Church, was built for Richard Chapel Whaley (1700–69) around 1765. He was a wealthy landowner from Whaley Abbey in Co. Wicklow. Anti-Catholic, Whaley was an enthusiastic priest-hunter. He was known as 'Burn-chapel' Whaley because once, while chasing a priest, he fired his gun into the thatched roof of a Catholic church, burning it to the ground.

Burn-chapel's eldest son, Thomas, who was better known as 'Buck' or 'Jerusalem', was only four years old when his father died in 1769. He inherited No. 86, as well as an annuity of £7,000 and a lump sum of £60,000. When Buck was only sixteen years old he was already living the life of a gambler and a rake, and he was sent to France to further his education in a futile attempt to put him back on the straight and narrow.

While getting his education in France, the young Buck also picked up some very bad habits and did his best to spend the family fortune in an endless round of drinking, gambling and debauchery. He returned to Dublin, but he soon grew restless and accepted a bet for £15,000 from his friends that he couldn't travel to Jerusalem and return to Dublin within the space of two years. He set off from Dublin on 20 September 1788 and, following a gruelling ten-month trip during which he was nearly killed by pirates and bandits, he arrived in Jerusalem.

While in the Holy Land, Buck made it his business to visit Ahmad Pasha al-Jazzar, a warlord known as 'the butcher', who was governor of the Ottoman Empire-controlled Damascus and Sidon.

One popular legend that arose out of Whaley's trip to the Holy Land was that he had agreed to play a game of handball against the walls of Jerusalem as a condition of the bet, but he doesn't make any reference to such an incident in his memoirs. He did, however, go to some lengths to provide proof that he had actually reached Jerusalem. His memoirs contain a copy of a signed certificate that he received from the superior of Terra Sancta in Jerusalem on 5 March 1789:

I the undersigned Guardian of this Convent of St. Mary, certify to all and singular who may read these presents, that

Messrs. Thomas Whaley and Hugh Moore have, on two occasions, been present and resided in this City of Nazareth for the space of three days, in witness whereof.[1]

Armed with this proof, Buck returned to Dublin to a hero's welcome in June or July of the following year, having fulfilled all the conditions of the bet. His friends reluctantly handed over the stake money of £15,000. The whole venture had cost him £8,000 and so he came out with a profit of £7,000. As Buck said in his memoirs, it was 'the only instance in all my life before, in which any of my projects turned out to my advantage'.[2]

Buck remained in Dublin for the next two years, drinking, gambling and generally living it up until the money ran out. He then went to London for a few years, where he became involved in several dubious enterprises and ended up in a debtors' prison in 1793. He was only freed when his brother-in-law and lord chancellor of Ireland 'Black Jack' Fitzgibbon agreed to pay off his debts for him.

Buck was elected MP for Newcastle, Co. Down, for a time and he also represented Enniscorthy. While MP for Enniscorthy, he accepted a bribe of £4,000 to vote for the Act of Union and subsequently accepted a similar sum to vote against it.

When Buck passed away on a visit to Cheshire in

England on 2 November 1800, the newspapers of the day reported that he had died from a 'rheumatic fever'. It was rumoured, however, that he had been stabbed to death by a jealous mistress who discovered that he had been engaged in an affair with her sister. He was buried at Knutsford in Cheshire and it was reported that just before he was placed in his coffin an Irish dancer named Robinson danced a hornpipe on the lid.

THE HOPKINS TOILET

The world-renowned poet and Jesuit priest Gerard Manley Hopkins was born in Essex, England, in 1844. He wrote his first poems when he was only fifteen and won a scholarship to study at Balliol College in Oxford. Hopkins, an Anglican, converted to the Catholic faith in 1866 and two years later joined the Jesuits. Following his ordination, he was sent to a number of parishes throughout England, but it soon emerged that he – who suffered from depression and was a poor public speaker – was totally unsuited for life as a preacher or a teacher.

Despite his failings, Hopkins was appointed professor of classics at the Catholic University (later University College Dublin) and moved to Dublin in 1884. He hated his life in Dublin and, shortly after his arrival in Stephen's Green, described his place of accommodation, Newman House, as a joyless and smoky ruin. Hopkins's bedroom and study were in the upper part of the house, next door to the University church and overlooking the south side of St Stephen's Green.

Hopkins remained very unsuited to the teaching profession and grumbled constantly about having to mark exam papers. On one occasion, after a marathon marking session, he complained bitterly, 'My eyes are almost bleeding … the feeling is like soap or lemons … the eyes are almost out of my head.'[3] This should have come as no surprise to the authorities at the Catholic University, as the head of the Jesuits who had sent him to Dublin wrote a letter to the president of the college saying, 'I should do you no kindness sending you a man so eccentric. I am trying him teaching this year, but with fear and trembling.'[4]

Hopkins soon fell into another depression and thought that he was possessed by the devil – he contemplated taking his own life. Unsurprisingly, given his mental state, Hopkins was completely unable to control the students and his classes often resembled riotous assemblies. The students teased him unmercifully; he was also disliked by the teaching staff, who had a very low opinion of his writing. One of his colleagues described his poetry as 'mere grammatical, acrobatic feats of jingling and word combination' that made his headaches worse, while another said that he suffered from a lack of judicial discernment and that his verses were a 'fantastic misuse of the English language'.[5]

Hopkins died from typhoid on 8 June 1889 in the basement area of Newman House. There was a bit of a furore in the halls of academia in the 1990s when it was discovered that the room where Hopkins died had been turned into a toilet. It was reported in the *Evening Press* that 'a group of visiting academics have reacted with outrage on discovering that the room where world-famous poet Gerard Manley Hopkins died is now being used as a toilet'.[6] A spokesman for Newman House told the reporter John Kilraine that Hopkins had only been put in there temporarily and it was not his normal room.

Hopkins was always a frail man during his life and he suffered from various ailments. However, many feel that the illness that finally killed him – typhoid – could have been avoided. His biographer, Dr Norman White, said that in the months following Hopkins's death £250 was raised to repair the water pipes at Newman House, which he said were discovered to be 'full of rats and filth', and he also said that the cook reported that two rats had been found swimming in a pot of stew.[7]

Still, for all his hardships, including the fact that his poetry was derided in his own lifetime, Hopkins did have the final laugh, as he is now considered to be one of the greatest poets of the Victorian era.

THE SHAM SQUIRE

One of the Green's most famous and definitely most un-scrupulous residents was the bold Francis Higgins, known to all and sundry as the Sham Squire. He lived at No. 72 St Stephen's Green, on the south side of the Green.

Higgins came from a poor background and was the son of a Co. Down man called Patrick Higgins and his wife, Mary. As a young man, Higgins worked at various jobs, including messenger boy, shoe shiner and waiter, before obtaining work in a solicitor's office in St Patrick's Close.

Higgins first came to public notoriety when he hood-winked Mary Anne Archer, daughter of a wealthy Dublin merchant, into marrying him. Higgins arranged a meeting with Mary Anne and her father using a priest as an intermediary, passing himself off as a gentleman and a nephew of an MP. The Protestant Higgins had also forged a legal document that portrayed him as a wealthy pro-perty owner and, crucially for the devoutly Catholic Mary Anne, stated that he had converted from Protestantism to Catholicism.

Mary Anne didn't find out that her husband was in fact a penniless chancer until it was too late. After the marriage, Higgins received a large dowry from his new father-in-law and also stood to inherit half of his wealth when he died. Upon finding out the deceit, Mary Anne returned to her parents' house, heartbroken. Higgins followed her and tried to gain entry to the house, during which he broke his new mother-in-law's arm. He was arrested and charged with assault. In the course of the trial a barrister referred to Higgins as a 'sham squire', a nickname that stayed with him for the rest of his life. Higgins was convicted for the assault on his mother-in-law, and also for an attack on a grocer, and he was sent to prison. Mary Anne died soon afterwards.

On his release from prison, Higgins set about spending his dead wife's money. He opened a tavern in Smock Alley with billiard and gambling tables. He quickly accumulated a small fortune smuggling tea to Dublin merchants and invested the money in a number of brothels. He also worked as a hosier on the side and became master of the Dublin hosiers' guild in 1775, which entitled him to a seat on Dublin Corporation. Five years later, he became an attorney, possibly with the help of his friend Attorney General John Scott, aka Copper-faced Jack. By various pieces of chicanery, Higgins managed to obtain the posts of deputy coroner of Dublin and under-sheriff of Dublin, and he also got himself appointed as a magistrate. He somehow wormed his way into a situation whereby he gained control of the influential opposition newspaper *The Freeman's Journal*.

The Freeman's Journal had originally been a radical newspaper when it was first published in 1763, but when

Higgins got his hands on it, the paper effectively became a tool of the British government. Higgins was rewarded for his loyalty by being given the lucrative business of publication of government proclamations. By the end of the 1780s he was one of the most influential men in the city.

Higgins became an extremely wealthy man and moved into a fashionable residence at No. 72 on the south side of St Stephen's Green, where:

> he was daily to be seen ... upon the Beaux Walk, in Stephen's Green, wearing a three-cocked hat fringed with swan's down, a canary-coloured vest, with breeches to match, a bright green body coat ... the only buck in Dublin who carried gold tassels on his Hessian boots, and violet gloves.[8]

However, it wasn't all plain sailing for the Sham Squire. Higgins clashed with John Magee, proprietor of the *Dublin Evening Post*. Magee, a Belfast radical, mounted a prolonged campaign to expose Higgins's corrupt behaviour.

Higgins once again turned to his friend Copper-faced Jack, aka Lord Clonmel, for assistance, and in 1790 he had Magee prosecuted under an obscure law for libel. Clonmel presided over the case himself and Magee, who didn't stand a chance, was convicted and thrown into Newgate

Prison. Perhaps some of Magee's accusations began to stick, however, as things began to go slightly awry for Higgins after that. He was sacked from his position as a magistrate the following year, and a few years after that he was struck off the legal rolls.

As it turns out, damningly, Higgins was also a spy for Dublin Castle. He secretly gave them information on the United Irishmen and in 1798 he was paid £1,000 for betraying Lord Edward Fitzgerald. Higgins died a wealthy man at his home at No. 72 Stephen's Green on 19 January 1802 and is buried at Kilbarrack graveyard.

THE IVEAGH GARDENS

Tucked away just to the south of St Stephen's Green are the Iveagh Gardens, one of Dublin's hidden jewels. The gardens originally belonged to the notorious judge Copper-faced Jack, who, when he wasn't hanging people, liked to hang out in his garden, where he planted exotic species from all over the world. It has been rumoured that there was an underground passage connecting Copper-faced Jack's house on Harcourt Street with the gardens, but there is no trace of a tunnel today.

At the end of the eighteenth century, the park was known as 'Lord Earlsfort's Lawn' after Copper-faced Jack's first title, Baron Earlsfort.

Arthur Guinness purchased the lands from a descendant of Copper-faced Jack in 1817 and opened them up to the public. When Guinness took over the gardens, they were in ruins. Sheep grazed there and the whole area was strewn with rubbish. Guinness brought in the famous gardener and landscape architect Ninian Niven to redesign the gardens in 1863. The Scottish-born Niven had previously been head gardener at the chief secretary

Restored waterfall at the Iveagh Gardens.

of Ireland's lodge in the Phoenix Park and curator at the Botanic Gardens in Glasnevin. He had also studied garden design in France and was renowned for his blended English and French gardening style.

Many of Niven's original features can still be seen in the gardens today and these include a water cascade, fountains, a maze and a rose garden. Another feature is the long sunken garden that was used for archery competitions.

*Restored ornamental fountain
at the Iveagh Gardens.*

When the gardens were first opened to the public, they were called the Coburg Gardens in honour of the British Queen Victoria's family, the Saxe-Coburgs. During that period, the gardens were a popular place of resort, and many events, such as firework displays, athletic events, concerts and exhibitions, were held there.

One novel sporting event that captured the public's imagination was the race that took place at the gardens on 18 May 1837 between the 'famous pedestrian' Cootes and a horse called Rover. Thousands gathered to witness the ten-mile race, which consisted of a course containing eighty hurdles and twenty walls.

Cootes was the 2–1 favourite at the outset of the contest and Rover was seen to be struggling right from the beginning, so much so that he had to be pulled up fifteen minutes into the race to be refreshed with water and brandy. *The Freeman's Journal* also reported that the poor horse, who refused a few of the jumps, was punished severely 'by a man with a pole' to encourage him over the fences. Some spectators also went out of their way to ensure Rover would lose, by wetting the fences as he tried to jump them and throwing water in his jockey's face to distract him. However, the horse and his rider – a man named Byrne – persisted and completed the course in fifty-six minutes, three minutes ahead of Cootes. Despite this, Cootes went on to claim the race on a technicality, as he was originally supposed to race against a mare of lesser ability than Rover.[9]

The Coburg Gardens were also a popular launchpad for balloonists. On 14 July 1824, William Wyndham Sadler took off from the gardens in a gas-filled balloon. The brown-and-yellow-striped balloon was filled with piped coal-fired gas supplied by the Hibernian Gas Company. The lord mayor of Dublin was there to see off Sadler – the first man to cross the Irish Sea in a balloon from Dublin to Holyhead in under five hours in 1812 – and his companion, Mr Levingston. In a speech that might have been directed at an astronaut flying to the moon in later years, Lady Manners, wife of the lord lieutenant, presented him with a flag, saying:

> *I sincerely hope you will have a safe, pleasant and prosperous excursion; and I shall be very glad, indeed, if the example of your enterprising spirit, shall be productive hereafter of advantages to your Country, by leading some useful discovery.*[10]

At 2 p.m., in front of a large crowd, the balloon was released and flew off in a northerly direction over the city and headed out over Dublin Bay towards Lambay Island. Sadler's excursion ended two hours later when he and his companion landed their balloon safely in a potato field near Rush in north Co. Dublin.

THE DUBLIN EXHIBITION PALACE AND WINTER GARDEN

The Coburg Gardens once hosted one of the largest industrial exhibitions ever held in Ireland.

For most of the nineteenth and the early part of the twentieth centuries, there were a number of international trade exhibitions held in Ireland, and in 1862 a committee comprised of noblemen and many of Dublin's leading businessmen, including Benjamin Lee Guinness and William Dargan, met to discuss the holding of an international trade exhibition in the city in order to promote trade and local industry. It was also proposed that the exhibition would contain a landscaped ornamental pleasure ground, a concert hall, reading and refreshment rooms, a public bazaar and a gymnasium.

The Dublin Exhibition Palace and Winter Garden Company proposed to set up an exhibition and a winter garden covered with an elaborate glass structure on the site of the Coburg Gardens. The foundation stone for the palace was laid on 12 June 1863 by the lord lieutenant and a sealed bottle containing some coins and copies of six Irish newspapers were buried beneath the foundation stone.

The building of the winter palace and the concert hall commenced soon afterwards and was complete by March 1865. Afterwards, the contractors came up with what seems, in modern times, to be a rather bizarre method of testing the strength of the building. The floorboards were tested by having several hundred workmen stamp on them at the one time. Soon afterwards, they were tested again by rolling thousands of cannon balls across them and, on 31 March, as a final safety check, 600 British soldiers belonging to the 78th Highlanders regiment in full pack and accompanied by the regimental band were marched around the entire floor space in double-quick time.

The exhibition was opened on 9 May 1865 by the Prince of Wales. Three thousand guests attended the opening ball given by the lord mayor at the Mansion House and the opening ceremony in the Concert Hall at Earlsfort Terrace featured a 500-strong choir.

By the time the exhibition closed, on 9 November 1865, nearly one million visitors had passed through its gates. Despite this it made little or no profit. A few smaller exhibitions were held on the site during the following years and in 1882 the buildings were sold to the government and became the Royal University of Ireland (now UCD), while the grounds remained in the hands of the Guinness family until they were taken over by the state in the 1990s.

The gardens became the Iveagh Gardens in 1865 and some of the original features from the winter palace, such as the cascade, fountain, rosarium and rustic grotto, have now been restored.

CECILIA BETHAM

Today, one of the few remaining original features of the Iveagh Gardens is the long narrow sunken garden on the St Stephen's Green side of the park. The pit was originally constructed as a venue for the Grand National Archery Fete at the winter garden exhibition in 1865. Thousands flocked there at the end of May every year to witness the best archers in Ireland and England battle it out for the top prizes.

The men's prize that first year was won by Mr G. Edwards of England and the ladies prize was won by Cecilia Betham, who won every competition in which she took part in England and Ireland during 1864 and 1865. Cecilia was Dublin and Ireland's very first female sports star.

Cecilia was the granddaughter of Sir William Betham, chief herald of Ireland, and she lived at Rockford in Blackrock, Co. Dublin. Her father was also a champion archer, as was her cousin Sheffield Betham, whom Cecilia later married. The Bethams were all members of the County of Dublin Archers club.

A year earlier, a writer in the Dublin *Daily Express* was glowing in his praise of Cecilia's skill with the longbow. A contest took place on that occasion at the Leinster Cricket Ground at Portobello in Dublin:

> *The shooting, as on the previous day, was excellent, and many of the competitors who had been rather low in score manifested a decided improvement in the number and value of the hits. The result, however, as to the leading prizes was never doubtful. Miss Betham maintained her superiority over the other ladies who competed, with much ease, her shooting being remarkable for the grace, coolness, and practised skill with which she performed her work on this occasion. This young lady is now the Champion of England, and, we may say, of Ireland also, the hitherto Champion of England, Mrs Horniblow, having yielded up that honour to Miss Betham's superior skill. Her performance during the present year has been somewhat remarkable, having made the highest score at the national meeting in Alexandra Park, London, also at the Sydenham and Leamington fetes, and secured the highest lady's prize given by the Royal Toxophilite Society, at their meeting lately held in the Regent's Park, by one of the highest recorded scores.*[11]

By 1872 Cecilia's influence in the world of archery was

on the wane, but she was still occasionally pulling top-drawer performances out of the bag, as evidenced by this report from the County Dublin Archers tournament at Monkstown Castle that year in *The Freeman's Journal*:

> *The lady has retained the premier position among the archers of the sister isle for five years, a career of triumph almost unparalleled in the records of championship, peaceful or otherwise. The other competitors were among the most famous who twang the bowstring in our modern 'sport of the gay greenwood'. As we have said, the shooting was wonderfully fine, a characteristic which might be anticipated from the first-rate calibre of those who contested. Miss Betham made the gross score of 336 and ten golds, an extraordinary feat, of which Robin Hood or William Tell themselves might be proud.*[12]

Cecilia Betham was so famous in her day that she had a dance, the Irish Archers' waltz, named in her honour; she also had an arrow named after her.

The Iveagh Gardens and Cecilia Betham are not the only interesting things about the environs south of the Green, however.

HARCOURT STREET

Today, Harcourt Street, leading southwards from Stephen's Green, is a modern and bustling street in the heart of the city, but a couple of centuries ago it was open countryside. For most of the nineteenth century it was known as Harcourt's Fields or Harcourt Street Fields. It was a place where Dubliners gathered for sporting activities and political rallies, but the city's criminal classes sometimes used it as a base to launch robberies and as a hiding place to stash their ill-gotten gains.

Harcourt Street and the fields before it were named after Simon Harcourt. A former lord lieutenant of Ireland, Harcourt drowned while trying to rescue his favourite dog from a well in 1777. When Harcourt was found, he was upside down with his legs sticking out of the well. The dog, meanwhile, was sitting on his feet, wet but alive.

The houses that you see today on Harcourt Street were, for the most part, built at the latter end of the eighteenth century. In 1777, a writer in *Saunders's News-Letter*, a Dublin newspaper, enthused about the development of the street:

> *The opening of Harcourt Street, at the south-west angle of St. Stephen's Green will make a noble avenue to that square, the greatest in Europe, which though not encompassed by such a number of sumptuous buildings as decorate those of Paris or London, surpasses any in these cities for its healthy and airy situation, and the living verdure it ever presents to the view. Harcourt Street (intended to pierce to the circular road) has already several elegant houses built in it, but none demands attention more than that elegant edifice erected by solicitor-general Scott; a mansion which for site, grandeur of design, finished taste, and excellence of execution, as a city residence, cannot be surpassed.*[13]

COPPER-FACED JACK

The 'solicitor-general Scott' mentioned in the newspaper article above – who has appeared in a handful of the stories told already in this book – was a man whose name would become, and still is, synonymous with Harcourt Street.

'Copper-faced' Jack Scott, Earl of Clonmel, lived at No. 14 Harcourt Street and is probably spinning in his grave – located in the vaults of St Luke's church in the Liberties – at the thought of his name being immortalised by a Harcourt Street nightclub.

Today, Copper Face Jack's nightclub in Harcourt Street has reached legendary status and is a Dublin – if not an

Irish – institution. When Dublin beat Kerry in an epic All-Ireland GAA football final at Croke Park in 2011, Bryan Cullen, captain of the Dublin team, ended his victory speech with the immortal line: 'See you all in Coppers.' There's even been a musical written about the nightclub.

Scott, the Tipperary-born 'hanging judge' and the first resident of Harcourt Street, was known as Copper-faced Jack because of his ruddy complexion, as well as his brazen behaviour. He was one of the nastiest, but most colourful characters of eighteenth-century Dublin. During a chequered career, he held the positions of solicitor general, attorney general, prime sergeant and lord chief justice, and finally ended up as Lord Clonmel.

Scott was a heavy drinker and, according to his neighbour Jonah Barrington, he was forever making resolutions to abstain from excessive 'snuff, sleep, swearing, gross eating, sloth, malt liquors and indolence,' and never to taste 'anything after tea but water, and wine and water at night'.[14] His good intentions never went anywhere, though, and he usually needed the help of a couple of able-bodied men to carry him home to his bed at night.

Scott was renowned for his arrogance and rudeness, and was hated by the majority of his colleagues at the Bar. In 1789, he abused a barrister by the name of Hackett so badly that his court was boycotted. Scott was forced to publish a substantial apology to Hackett in the newspapers.

He had a particular dislike for the clergy, especially bishops, whom he described as being hypocritical and greedy. He also despised musicians, describing them as fools in mind and conduct.

In turn, Copper-faced Jack was himself despised by many and he became a target of public anger for his unwavering support of the government and his opposition to public causes. On one occasion, he narrowly escaped death when, during a riot on 15 November 1779, a mob armed with swords and pistols besieged his Harcourt Street home.

Scott was involved in a long-running feud with John Magee, proprietor of the *Dublin Evening Post*, which began after the judge held Magee in custody on a charge of libel to a very excessive bail of £4,000, a huge sum in those days. It was believed at the time that Scott bore ill-will against Magee for having personally abused him in his paper.

Magee, who was also known for his erratic behaviour, swore to get even with Scott and, on his release from Newgate Prison, had posters erected around Dublin stating that he had £14,000, £10,000 of which he had settled upon his family, and it was his intention to spend the balance on getting his revenge on Lord Clonmel.

As well as his mansion at Harcourt Street, Scott owned a villa called Temple Hill near Seapoint in Co. Dublin. As part of his revenge, Magee bought a plot of land right next door to Temple Hill and erected posters inviting his fellow citizens to join him in 'days of great amusement' to be held there every weekend.[15]

Thousands turned up for these events, which included musical entertainment provided by pipers and harpers. Sport featured prominently on these days of amusement, the most popular events being football and cudgelling. Cudgelling can best be described as a duel fought with wooden sticks in which the object was to smash your opponent's head open. The first man to draw blood won the contest.

The games at Temple Hill usually began with a football match involving the entire crowd, who used a bladder filled with foetid gas as a ball. These were possibly the biggest football matches ever seen in Ireland.

Lord Cloncurry, who lived near Temple Hill, attended one of these gatherings and made the following observations:

Several thousand people, including the entire disposable mob of Dublin, of both sexes, assembled as the guests at an early hour in the morning, and proceeded to enjoy themselves in tents and booths erected for the occasion. A variety of sports were arranged for their amusement, such as climbing poles for prizes, running in sacks, grinning through horse-collars, asses dressed up with wigs and scarlet robes, dancing dogs in gowns and

wigs as barristers, and so forth, until at length, when the crowd
had obtained its maximum density, towards the afternoon, the
grand scene of the day was produced.

A number of active pigs, with their tails shaved and soaped,
were let loose, and it was announced that each pig should become
the property of any one who could catch and hold it by the slippery
member. A scene impossible to describe immediately took place; the
pigs, frightened and hemmed in by the crowd in all directions,
rushed through the hedge which then separated Temple Hill from
the open fields; forthwith all their pursuers followed in a body,
and continuing their chase over the shrubberies and parterres,
soon revenged John Magee upon the noble owner.[16]

The star of the show that day was apparently a fat pig
that Magee had christened 'Shamado' after Copper-faced
Jack's friend and neighbour the Sham Squire, Francis
Higgins.[17] These gatherings were of great annoyance to
Copper-faced Jack, but they were not riotous enough to
be deemed a public nuisance as they were held on Magee's
own land, which Clonmel had neglected to purchase when
he built his house.

Scott eventually had the last laugh, however, when
he jailed the increasingly eccentric Magee for nineteen
months for contempt of court.

Copper-faced Jack Scott died at the age of fifty-nine
on the day the 1798 rebellion broke out, 23 May. He was

buried in St Peter's church in Aungier Street, which was later demolished to make way for the YMCA centre. Scott's remains, along with the others buried at St Peter's, were transferred to St Luke's in the Liberties.

Perhaps the last word on Scott should be left to Copper-faced Jack's Harcourt Street neighbour Jonah Barrington, who described him as:

> *Courageous, vulgar, humorous, he knew the world well and he profited by that knowledge. He cultivated the powerful; he bullied the timid; he fought the brave; he flattered the vain; he duped the credulous; and he amused the convivial ... Half-liked, half-reprobated, he was too high to be despised and too low to be respected.*[18]

HARCOURT STREET FIELDS

Throughout the early part of the nineteenth century, the area was constantly in the news as the city authorities fought the lower orders for control over Harcourt Street Fields. An editorial in *The Freeman's Journal* in January 1821 called on the city magistrates to take action against what it called:

> *the groups of dissolute persons of both sexes, who are in the habit of daily and nightly assembling in the fields adjacent to the town end of Harcourt-street, and the tract of ground which*

is intended to be converted into a street leading to Fitzwilliam square.[19]

The writer complained that no decent woman could walk there because of:

the indecent conduct of the prostitutes who infest the neighbourhood, and who are always attended by a gang of the other sex, who at night and in the dusk of the evening, join them in committing acts of violence and outrage on the passengers ...[20]

He also called on the magistrates and police to enforce the observance of the Sabbath in the area and crack down on the gangs who gathered there every Sunday:

for the purpose of boxing, wrestling, kicking foot ball, &c. The noise, riot, blasphemy, and obscene language, (not to mention personal danger), has rendered residence in the vicinity extremely uncomfortable.[21]

One such outrage occurred at Harcourt Street Fields in September 1822, when a three-year-old boy from Thomas Street was found naked there. The crime of child-stripping was a fairly common one in Dublin at that time. Clothing was expensive and there was a thriving second-hand market for quality items in the city. Typically, well-dressed children were the preferred target of child-strippers and the perpetrators were usually women who would lure the child with the promise of sweets or perhaps a toy. The child would then be taken to a remote location, stripped of all its clothing and abandoned.

On this occasion, the boy, the son of a well-to-do merchant from Thomas Street, was kidnapped outside his father's house and brought to Harcourt Street Fields, where he was stripped and left to fend for himself. It was reported in *The Freeman's Journal* that the child would have perished had it not been for a gentleman who heard him crying and brought him to College Street Police Station (now Pearse Street railway station). The boy could barely talk, but he was able to tell them that he was from Thomas Street. The police brought him to the street where, after some enquiries, he was reunited with his parents.[22]

In March 1831 the *Dublin Evening Post* reported that hundreds had assembled at Harcourt Street Fields for a hurling match. The police were called and attempted to stop the game, but the crowd turned on them and gave them a severe beating. The riot was only quelled with the arrival of the city's horse police and several of the crowd were arrested and committed to trial.[23]

In a conflicting report about this incident, another newspaper claimed that 500 people had been playing football at the venue when Constable Fletcher of the Dublin Metropolitan Police tried to slash the ball with his sword. The crowd retaliated, attacking the police with sticks and stones, and six policemen were seriously injured in the rioting that followed. One policeman named Harris was badly injured when one of the rioters took his sword away from him and wounded him severely in the head and neck. Several rioters were taken into custody, but they were subsequently released due to lack of evidence.[24]

In early May 1833, Harcourt Street Fields were the venue for a boxing match between two chimney sweeps: Dan Connell and Peter Boaten, who lived in the Bow Lane, Mercer Street area, which was known locally as the 'Holy Land'.

Connell was a well-known character in the area because of his fondness for fighting and he had seen the inside of Dublin's police stations on many occasions. A Catholic, he was affectionately known to his friends as 'The Liberator' after his namesake Daniel O'Connell.

Dan's opponent on that occasion was Peter 'Bully' Boaten, an Orangeman who was handy with his fists. The fight came about after a drunken Dan arrived home late one night to find Boaten in bed with his wife. The two men squared up to each other on the street and they had to be separated by a strong detachment of the Dublin Metropolitan Police.

A proper fight was arranged for the next evening at Harcourt Street Fields, just outside the wall of the Coburg Gardens. Connell was seconded by one of his neighbours, who was known as 'the general', while Boaten was seconded by a farrier known locally as 'the doctor'. Dan wore green shorts with a sprig of shamrock under his belt, while his rival wore orange and blue colours.

The two chimney sweeps slugged it out for a gruelling twenty rounds in front of a large crowd of spectators, and they were just about to start the twenty-first when a party of police jumped over the wall from the Coburg Gardens and broke up the fight. According to the newspaper reports, the fight had been fairly even up to that point. One newspaper reported that, by the end of it, the two protagonists were 'bleeding like pigs, but, nevertheless, were determined to fight it out to the last'. A rematch was arranged for a later date, but the outcome of that is not known.[25]

As the nineteenth century progressed, Harcourt Street Fields were gradually built over and that put paid to most of the trouble. However, there was another major riot there in 1878, when a dozen soldiers of the Wicklow Artillery Militia reserve ran amok at what was left of Harcourt Street Fields. At one stage, the rioting was so intense that all businesses in the area were forced to close, trams were halted and the front entrance of Harcourt Street railway station was locked to prevent the soldiers from entering.

The old Harcourt railway station was the scene of a major riot in 1878.

The soldiers had been hanging around Harcourt Street and drinking all that morning. When they were ordered by their superiors to board a train bound for the south, they refused and instead began to march around the top of Harcourt Street and Harrington Street, stopping off frequently to slake their thirst in several public houses.

The company sergeant enlisted the aid of the Dublin Metropolitan Police and a number of constables headed by a Sergeant Laracy arrived to try to calm matters. However, the presence of the police only served to inflame the situation, and Laracy, who was known on the streets of Dublin as 'Madden's Baby', was savagely beaten by the soldiers. The police were aided in their endeavours to arrest the soldiers by 'some respectable citizens', but a number of Dubliners, described as 'roughs' from the lanes and alleyways around Aungier Street and Camden Street, weighed in on the side of the soldiers and helped them in their attack on the police.[26]

During the fighting, the militiamen were heard to shout that they would rather be sent to Spike Island (an island prison in Cork harbour) than fight for the 'bloody British government', while another was heard to say that he would rather fight with a bobby than with a Russian.

The riot eventually ended with the arrival of police reinforcements. Six of the soldiers were arrested and the other six were escorted under military guard to Portobello Barracks and lodged in the guardroom.[27]

The commander of the Wicklow Artillery Militia – the aptly named Colonel Gun Cuninghame – gave glowing character references for his men, but, despite that, two of the ringleaders were found guilty of riot and assault and were sentenced to two months' imprisonment with hard labour, while the other four were sentenced to a month with hard labour.

LEONARD McNALLY

No. 22 Harcourt Street was the home of the United Irishman, barrister, writer and informer Leonard McNally.

McNally was the son of a grocer from Mary's Lane and he tried his hand at his father's trade before it ended in bankruptcy in 1772. He studied law in London and was called to the Irish Bar in 1776 but returned to London where he worked as a journalist and wrote plays for the London stage. The best-known and most successful of these was 'Robin Hood, or, Sherwood Forest, a comic opera', released in 1784.

Before returning to Dublin in 1790, McNally was called to the English Bar and practised law for a time. On his return to Ireland he joined the Dublin Society of United Irishmen, of which he was one of the original members. He frequently appeared in court on behalf of Theobald Wolfe Tone, Robert Emmet, Napper Tandy and others.

McNally was friendly with the French spy William Jackson, who was assessing the possibilities for a French invasion of Ireland. He set up meetings for McNally with some of the leading lights of the United Irishmen, such as Wolfe Tone and Archibald Hamilton Rowan. Jackson's travelling companion was a man named John Cockayne and it was subsequently discovered that Cockayne was an informer. Jackson was charged with high treason for his activities and Cockayne gave evidence against him in court, which ultimately cost Jackson his life.

It is believed that McNally was compromised by his

relationship with Cockayne and turned informer in 1794 or 1795. He passed information to Dublin Castle on his fellow United Irishmen from that point on and was regarded as one of their best agents.

Wearing his legal hat, McNally was involved in several important cases, including the trials of William Jackson and of the brothers John and Henry Sheares for treason. He also gave information to Dublin Castle in relation to the attempted French landing at Bantry Bay in 1796, where Wolfe Tone was captured.

McNally still kept up his public front of being a United Irishmen supporter. He even went so far as to fight a duel in the Phoenix Park in 1794 with his neighbour Jonah Barrington because the latter had insulted the United Irishmen.

> *McNally stood before me, very like a beer barrel on its stilling and by his side were ranged three unfortunate barristers, who were all soon afterwards hanged and beheaded for high treason – namely, John Sheares, who was his second, and Henry Sheares and Bagenal Harvey who came as amateurs.*[28]

Barrington shot McNally and he fell to the ground, crying out, 'I'm hit.' The doctor in attendance rushed to help McNally and discovered that the bullet had hit him in the buckle of his suspenders. He exclaimed, according to Barrington, 'By Jaysus Mac! you are the only rogue I ever knew that was saved by the gallows.'[29] (Gallows was a common term at that time for suspenders.) As Barrington mentioned, the Sheares brothers were later hanged and beheaded for high treason, on 14 July 1798.

The account written by Barrington himself is amusing on one level, but also quite poignant, in that McNally had clearly been friends with the Sheares, but ultimately that friendship meant nothing when McNally sold them and others out for a pension.

McNally died at his home on Harcourt Street in mid-February 1820, but his role as an informer wasn't revealed until well after his death, with the publication of R. R. Madden's second edition of *The United Irishmen: Their Lives and Times* in 1857. Details documenting McNally's double-dealing appeared when a manuscript called the 'Secret Service Money Book' came to light. The book had been held in Dublin Castle and details payments made to castle spies and informants between 1797 and 1804. It is believed that the book came into the public domain when a carpenter working in Dublin Castle stole it and sold it to a shopkeeper in Capel Street. Madden later published extracts from it in his book.

The book showed that McNally had been receiving £300 annually from 1798 up until his death for his work as a government spy. This included keeping a close eye on members of the United Irishmen and Robert Emmet, the leader of the failed rebellion of 1803 in Dublin. He sent regular reports to his handler at Dublin Castle on Emmet's movements, such as in 1800 when he reported to under-secretary Edward Cook that 'Emmet junior' had travelled to France on business. The two-faced McNally even defended Emmet during his famous trial in September 1803. The money book reveals that he received £100 on the day of Emmet's capture and another £100 five days before the trial.

Emmet was duly tried and sentenced to death. On the morning of Emmet's execution, McNally was the only one allowed to visit him. Emmet's mother had just died, but no one had told Emmet. When he asked if he could see her, McNally broke the news to him by pointing up at the sky saying, 'Robert, you shall meet her this day.'[30]

THE GREEN TUREEN MURDER

Few people in Ireland had ever heard of Hazel Mullen or her boyfriend Shan Mohangi when she went missing in the middle of August 1963. But within days all that was to change.

To this day Dubliners still recall the dashing twenty-two-year-old College of Surgeons student who was subsequently convicted of killing sixteen-year-old Hazel. He strangled her and cut up her body with a meat cleaver

from the kitchen of The Green Tureen. Seventeen different parts of the young Shankill girl's body were found by
police in the basement of the restaurant at 95 Harcourt
Street. Knives, cleavers and blood told the horror of what
had occurred on Saturday 17 August 1963.

The Irish Press of Wednesday 21 August carried a front-
page story recounting the events at 95 Harcourt Street,
dramatically relating how the owner of the building, Cecil
Frew, raised the alarm after Mohangi confessed to him.
Sergeant James Connell was the first Garda officer at the
scene and told how he approached the student's flat on
the second-floor landing:

> *I could see the light was on. I knocked twice and got no reply.
> Then I smelled the gas, and heard it running in the room. We
> forced the door and when I entered I saw Mohangi lying on a
> bed apparently asleep. I turned off two gas jets, one on a cooker,
> and one on a gas fire, pulled back the curtains and opened both
> windows.*[31]

In an attempt to end his own life Mohangi had taken
tablets and tried to gas himself, but he subsequently recovered and on Monday 10 February 1964 he went on
trial for Hazel's murder. Sixteen days later, a jury found
him guilty and he was sentenced to death. Mohangi immediately appealed against the sentence. In his statement

to gardaí, Mohangi said that he and Hazel had planned to get engaged. On that fateful Saturday she had finished work at Brown's Chemist in Stephen's Green at 12.30 and had arrived at No. 95 for lunch between 1.00 and 1.05 p.m.

> *She asked me if she could see the place. I brought her down and showed her all over the basement. She told me in the basement that she had something to do with somebody else. She did not mention the person's name but she said it was sex. I don't know what happened me ...* [32]

Mohangi continued:

> *I was raging at this time. I got hold of her by the neck and put my hands around her neck, and before I knew anything it was the end ... I did not intend killing Hazel. The moment I learned she was unfaithful to me I lost my head and did something rash which I am regretting now.* [33]

In January 1965, at a re-trial, Mohangi was found guilty of the lesser offence of manslaughter and was sentenced to seven years in jail. He served just three years of his sentence before he was deported to South Africa, where he lives in Natal with his wife and three children. He dropped the name Mohangi, which had become so infamous in

Ireland, and adopted the name Shan Jamuma, a family name from his mother's side.

In 1984 he stood for election in the Asians-only chamber of South Africa's Tricameral Parliament and won a seat for the Natal province. However, after the apartheid system crumbled, he was unsuccessful when he stood for election for the National Party.

In 1994 he gave an interview to an RTÉ camera crew for the highly successful *Thou Shalt Not Kill* series. As he recalled that awful night of thirty years previously, his voice broke and he had difficulty articulating his remorse. 'If I had one wish, it would be to bring Hazel Mullen back and undo what has been done. But that is not possible,' he said.

Hazel's mother Bridget later forgave Mohangi, saying: 'I bear no grudge and wish him well.' Her son Ian added, 'Not only have we forgiven Shan, but in our view God has forgiven him.'[34]

DRACULA

No. 16 Harcourt Street was once the home of one of Dublin's, if not the world's, most famous writers – Bram Stoker, author of *Dracula*. In terms of sales, *Dracula* has made Bram Stoker one of the bestselling authors of all time. Over the years, Stoker's classic has been the basis for countless films and has spawned a huge industry.

Abraham or 'Bram' Stoker was born at No. 15 Marino

Crescent, Fairview, in November 1847. He was the third of seven children and his father was a civil servant at Dublin Castle. During his childhood, Stoker was afflicted by sickness and ill health, and he spent the first eight years of his life in bed, unable to walk or even stand. One of Stoker's earliest influences was his mother, Charlotte Thornley, who regaled him with tales of the 1832 cholera epidemic in her native Sligo. One tale that particularly affected the young Stoker was his mother's story of a traveller who was struck down with cholera some distance from the town. The locals, fearing for their own safety, pushed the stranger into a pit with long sticks and buried him alive.

By the time he attended Trinity College in 1864, Stoker had grown out of his childhood illnesses and become an athlete of some note. He was also president of the Philosophical Society and auditor of the Historical Society. On graduation, he entered the civil service but soon found that it was not to his liking. He became interested in the theatre and worked as an unpaid theatre critic for the *Dublin Evening Mail*.

In 1876, when the famous actor Sir Henry Irving played Hamlet in Dublin, Stoker reviewed the play. Irving was impressed by the review and extended him an invitation to become manager of the Lyceum Theatre in London.

Stoker moved to Harcourt Street sometime around 1876. He married his neighbour and one-time girlfriend of Oscar Wilde, Florence Balcombe, at St Ann's church in Dawson Street in 1878. The couple soon moved to London, taking up Irving's offer. The two became firm friends and Stoker remained at the Lyceum for the next thirty years, managing the day-to-day running of the theatre and acting as Irving's personal secretary.

Stoker's first book was a little-known work entitled *The Duties of Clerks of Petty Sessions in Ireland*. His most famous work, *Dracula*, published in 1897, was inspired by another Dubliner, Sheridan Le Fanu, and his classic vampire tale *Carmilla*, which had been written twenty-five years earlier.

Stoker began research on the Dracula story in 1890. He had originally called the book 'Count Wampyr', but later changed the title to 'Dracula', the Romanian word for devil. Unfortunately for Stoker, the book was not initially popular with the British public and didn't sell many copies. It received mixed reviews in the British press, and the *Daily Mail* described it as being even more appalling than either *Frankenstein* or *Wuthering Heights*. However, Bram's mother loved the book and wrote to her son, saying: 'My dear, it is splendid, a thousand miles beyond anything you have written before, and I feel certain will place you high in the writers of the day.'[35]

Dracula eventually achieved decent sales figures in America, but Stoker had neglected to secure the copyright, so didn't receive a penny for his efforts.

Following his friend Irving's death in 1906, Stoker published *Personal Reminiscences of Henry Irving*. In 1911 his last book, *The Lair of the White Worm*, appeared. Stoker fell into ill health shortly afterwards and died on 20 April 1912. He was buried at Golders Green cemetery in London.

***

These days, Harcourt Street has taken over from Leeson Street as the number-one venue for clubbers. With a string of nightclubs including Coppers, Diceys, Krystle and others, the long lines of punters queuing to get in from an early hour are a familiar sight on the street. Some of the beautiful old Georgian houses have now sadly been replaced by office blocks, but, despite that, Harcourt Street today is still one of the most fashionable thoroughfares in the capital city.

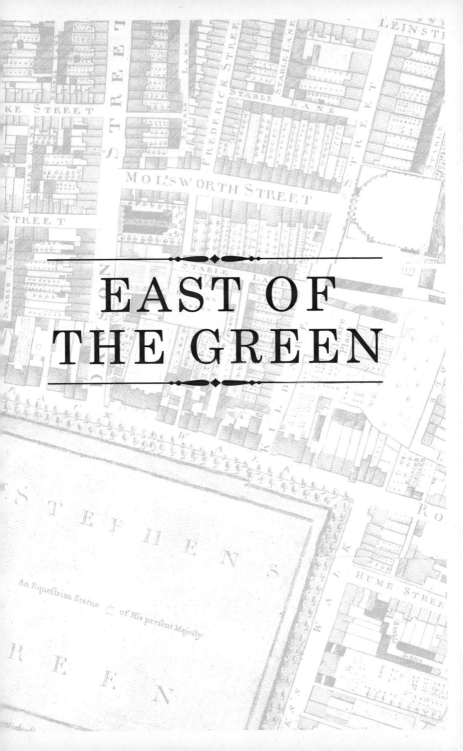

EAST OF
THE GREEN

BAGGOT
STREET

Baggot Street was originally laid out in 1773 and is named after Sir Robert Baggot (spelled 'Bagod' in some sources), who was lord chief justice in Ireland at the time. It was he who built Baggotrath Castle, which played a big role in the 1641 rebellion. The castle was the venue for the defining battle of the conflict that took place between the Cromwellian army and the royalists led by the Duke of Ormonde. There's nothing left of the castle today, but the site once occupied by it is now 44–46 Baggot Street opposite Waterloo Road. The street was called the Gallows Road during the eighteenth century and it led directly from St Stephen's Green to Baggotrath Castle.

THE SHEARES BROTHERS

No. 128 Lower Baggot Street was the home of the United Irishmen John and Henry Sheares, who were hanged for high treason in 1798. The Cork-born brothers, both barristers, had visited France during the French Revolution in 1792, where they met some of the leading

No. 128 Lower Baggot Street was the home of the United Irishmen John and Henry Sheares.

lights of the revolution, as well as Lord Edward Fitzgerald and William Jackson.

When they returned to Dublin, the brothers joined the Dublin Society of United Irishmen. John was the more militant of the two and played a leading role in organising the 1798 rebellion. He also effectively took over the leadership of the rebellion after Lord Edward Fitzgerald went into hiding.

The end came for the Sheares brothers in May 1798 after John had the misfortune to meet a man named John Warneford Armstrong in Patrick Byrne's bookshop in Grafton Street. He tried to recruit him for the rebellion. Despite being a known captain in the King's County militia, Armstrong was trusted because he had been a pupil at Samuel Whyte's Academy in Grafton Street and had spent long hours in Byrne's bookshop buying radical publications and expressing views that were favourable to the United Irishmen.

However, Armstrong was in fact an informer. After agreeing to defect to the United Irishmen, along with his regiment, Armstrong went straight back to his commanding officer, Henry L'Estrange, and told him everything. L'Estrange advised him to play along with the scheme.

Over the following weeks, Armstrong met both brothers at their home in Baggot Street to discuss the rebellion and also discussed a plan to seize the British military base at Loughlinstown outside Dublin. Armstrong of course was feeding all of this information back to L'Estrange.

The brothers were arrested on 21 May, two days before the outbreak of the rebellion. John was arrested at the home of another United Irishman, William Lawless, in French Street, while Henry was taken at their home in Baggot Street. A proclamation in John's handwriting was discovered during the raid at Baggot Street and both brothers were subsequently charged with high treason.

The trial took place on 12 July and they were swiftly convicted. Dressed in black, the Sheares brothers walked to the scaffold together, holding hands, and were hanged at Newgate Prison on 14 July in front of a large crowd. After hanging, the brothers were beheaded and their remains were taken to the nearby St Michan's church and interred in a vault. The Sheares brothers were the first of the leaders of the United Irishmen to be executed.

It emerged afterwards that a last-ditch attempt to save

Henry's life – as he was the less militant of the brothers – failed. The lord chancellor, John Fitzgibbon, who had once been a love rival of Henry's, decreed that he would spare him if he agreed to give information to the authorities, but the letter arrived at Newgate too late to save him. We'll never know if Henry would have agreed to those terms.

FERGUSON'S GARAGE

One of the first actions of the Irish Civil War took place on 26 June 1921, at No. 134 Lower Baggot Street, when a group of anti-Treaty soldiers led by Leo Henderson turned up to confiscate a number of cars at the premises, which was then Ferguson's Garage. The anti-Treaty IRA was enforcing a boycott on southern firms doing business with Belfast firms, in response to the violence being inflicted on nationalists there, and four cars were to be seized from Ferguson's as a reprisal for their breaking the boycott.

No. 134 Lower Baggot Street is the site of Ferguson's Garage, where one of the first actions of the Irish Civil War took place on 26 June 1921.

Henderson was just about to commandeer the cars and take them to the anti-Treaty headquarters at the Four Courts when he was captured by Free State troops. In response, the anti-Treaty side, led by Ernie O'Malley, kidnapped the pro-Treaty Lieutenant General J. J. 'Ginger' O'Connell and held him as a hostage at the Four Courts, saying O'Connell would only be released in exchange for Henderson. In retaliation, the Free State army readied themselves to attack the Four Courts, the shelling ultimately being carried out over a period of three days from 28 to 30 June.

WATERLOO HOUSE

Waterloo House, a bar now called The Waterloo at No. 36 Upper Baggot Street, was one of writer Brian O'Nolan's favourite haunts. He had the strange habit of carrying a whiskey measure with him so that he could check to see that he wasn't being short-changed by the publican. O'Nolan was better known by his noms de plume of

The Waterloo bar.

Flann O'Brien and Myles na gCopaleen, and his writings include his classic works *At-Swim-Two-Birds*, *The Third Policeman* and the Irish-language novel *An Béal Bocht*.

The Waterloo bar was famous for being one of the city's first pubs to have a lounge bar, and was opened in 1932 by the mayor of Dublin, Alfie Byrne. The lounge caused some controversy because it had a ladies toilet and it was claimed that this would only encourage women to drink in pubs.

The poet Patrick Kavanagh, who lived nearby, was a regular visitor, as was the poet Michael Hartnett. The Dubliners were also regulars at The Waterloo and Brendan Behan was known to drop in on the odd occasion.

GAJ'S RESTAURANT

Margaret Gaj's restaurant at No. 132 Lower Baggot Street was a popular Dublin eatery in the 1960s and 1970s. The haunt of revolutionaries and left-wingers, it was the headquarters of the Irish Women's Liberation Movement, of which Margaret Gaj was treasurer.

Margaret Gaj (née Dunlop) was born in Edinburgh in 1919 and she came to Ireland in 1947 with her husband Boleslaw Gaj, a Polish soldier whom she had met while working at a Scottish hospital as a nurse during the Second World War.

Margaret opened a restaurant in Molesworth Street

and moved afterwards to Baggot Street. The restaurant was known for its reasonable prices and there were no airs and graces. The menu was a simple one and included burgers, chips, tea and toast. She ran a democratic shop: staff were hired for a trial period, at the end of which the other staff would vote on whether the probationer should stay or go.

Margaret was a dedicated political activist and one of her favourite causes was the Prisoners' Rights Organisation. She and her son were once sentenced to a year in jail for picketing a court in order to highlight the case of a prisoner who had made several attempts to commit suicide. The sentence was reduced on appeal and the Probation Act was applied instead.

Margaret Gaj's restaurant, haunt of Dublin's left-wingers and revolutionaries in the 1970s.

The restaurant closed its doors for the last time in 1980. When she died in 2011, Margaret

Gaj was described in *The Irish Times* as a 'kind-hearted and formidable woman who passionately believed in the right to protest'.[1] Fellow member of the Irish Women's Liberation Movement Máirín de Burca said of her:

> *A whole generation of political activists have reason to be grateful to Margaret Gaj – not just for her unfailing personal and, at times, financial support – but for the home-away-from-home atmosphere furnished by the restaurant.*[2]

PARSONS BOOKSHOP

Parsons Bookshop on Baggot Street Bridge is sadly no longer with us, but, in its heyday, the shop was one of Dublin's leading literary landmarks. Literary heavy hitters such as Frank O'Connor, Brendan Behan, Liam O'Flaherty, Mary Lavin and Seamus Heaney were all regular visitors, while the poet Patrick Kavanagh made it his second home. Mary Lavin once said of the bookshop that there were more writers to be seen on the shop floor than there were on the bookshelves.

Kavanagh visited the shop on most mornings, perching himself on a stool that he referred to as his milking stool. Once ensconced on his throne, Kavanagh would help himself to a free read of the newspapers and catch up on the previous day's racing results in the British red tops.

Brendan Behan was also a regular visitor to the shop.

Parsons Bookshop on Baggot Street Bridge was one of the city's best-known bookshops and it was regularly frequented by literary heavyweights such as Brendan Behan and Patrick Kavanagh.

The proprietor, May O'Flaherty, recalled that he was in the shop one day when a priest and his mother came in to look for books. Behan observed them for a while before quipping to the proprietor: 'Only in Ireland will you hear a mother call her son father.'[3]

On another occasion Behan arrived into Parsons, picked up the *Catholic Herald* and exclaimed, 'Ah, the news of the next world.'[4]

The bookshop was opened in 1949 by O'Flaherty, who ran it for many years with her assistant, May King, until its closure in 1989.

***

Nowadays, the upper and lower parts of Baggot Street are distinguished by their differing architecture, with Lower Baggot Street being primarily made up of Georgian-era planning, while Upper Baggot Street consists mainly of Victorian architecture, along with some prominent twentieth-century buildings. The street is also now known for its many pubs, and is a popular location for the Twelve Pubs of Christmas pub crawl every holiday season.

WEST OF
THE GREEN

YORK
STREET

The York Street of today bears no resemblance to the original version of the street, as most of the old dwellings are gone. Connecting St Stephen's Green to Aungier Street, the street was first developed in 1673 by the Aungier estate and, according to C. T. McCready, it was named after Ernest Augustus, Duke of York and Albany.

It was once one of Dublin's most fashionable streets and it used to lead to the original entrance to St Stephen's Green park to the west of the Green. For much of the nineteenth century York Street was home to many of Dublin's medical profession, with elegant town houses on both sides of the street. In addition, there were a number of small specialist hospitals and medical facilities, such as the Dublin Ear and Throat Hospital and the Eye and Ear Hospital. The other institutions in York Street with medical associations were the Southern Cow Pock Institution, the Cholera Orphan Society and a dental hospital. York Street was also the birthplace of many of the city's leading doctors.

CONSERVATIVE WORKINGMEN'S CLUB RIOT

Just off St Stephen's Green, the Conservative Working-men's Club (CWC) had a membership of around 300 and was mainly frequented by working-class Protestants. It also housed one of Dublin's biggest Orange halls. The club was founded in 1883 and its first president was Edward Guinness of the famous brewing family. Some of Dublin's leading Orangemen were patrons of the CWC, as was the leading British Tory Randolph Churchill.

Membership of the club was open to Protestant men of a Conservative persuasion and one of its stated aims was to improve the lives of the Protestant working classes.

York Street, where a major riot took place at the Conservative Workingmen's Club in 1886.

To that end the CWC had a library, held educational lectures, ran dances and concerts, and organised excursions. The biggest draw, though, was the club's bar and billiard room.

The bar had a reputation for hard-drinking clientele, and violence was a fairly common occurrence. During the general election campaigns of 1885 and 1886, for example, the CWC became the focus for serious political violence between Irish nationalists who sought to break the connection with Britain and the loyalists who wanted to maintain it. On the night of 28 November 1885, the club was wrecked during the election campaign. The Nationalist York Street Club, which was only a few doors away from the CWC, demanded the removal of a large Union Jack flag and bunting from a window. When the request was refused, the nationalists attacked the CWC and completely destroyed it.

However, that incident paled in comparison to the riot that took place at the club on the night of 5 July 1886, during which one man died, at least fifty were injured and eighty-five were arrested by the city police. The rioting occurred following the election of the nationalist candidate Edmund Dwyer Gray as MP for the St Stephen's Green ward of Dublin city.

At about eight o'clock in the evening, bands celebrating Gray's victory began to parade in the area and soon attracted a huge crowd. Later an estimated 2,000–3,000 of Gray's supporters converged on the CWC.

The bands came to a halt outside the club, which was packed with Orangemen, and began to play a selection of rousing Fenian tunes. When asked later to describe exactly what these tunes were, Police Inspector Talbot said that he didn't know but commented wryly that he was sure they weren't playing 'God save the Queen'.

When the nationalists began to sing 'God save Ireland', the Orangemen inside the club responded by booing and hissing. The crowd then began to hurl bottles, stones and bricks at the building, and an unsuccessful attempt was made to set the front door on fire.

At the height of the rioting, a number of shots were discharged from inside the CWC and some of the demonstrators were taken to the nearby Mercer's Hospital with gunshot wounds. One man, James McConn, died while running from the scene directly after the shooting, but it was established afterwards that he had died from a heart attack.

The crowd quickly dispersed after the shooting and a large force of police entered the Conservative Club. They arrested eighty-five Orangemen, most of them armed with cudgels. Fourteen rioters were arrested outside the club, but were not detained. Inside the club, police discovered a number of iron bars and, in a yard at the back of the house, they uncovered two revolvers that had recently been fired and a quantity of ammunition.

Three Dublin Orangemen – Archibald Cruickshank, Robert Clarke and William Ward – were charged with firing into the crowd, but were later acquitted, as were the others arrested in the CWC.

Sporadic rioting continued around the city for the next three nights. On 7 July large numbers of nationalists again gathered in York Street, this time to defend the nationalist club against attack from the students of Trinity College, who had threatened to 'capture the Fenian flag in York Street'.[1] The students never carried out their threat, although they were involved in a few minor incidents throughout the city.

The bell ringers of St Patrick's Cathedral had the last word in the matter at midnight on 8 July. After ringing the midnight hour, they rang out the tune of 'Rule Britannia' just after midnight. However, no one responded to this act of provocation and the streets remained calm.

The Conservative Workingmen's Club on York Street has long since been demolished to make way for an extension to the Royal College of Surgeons.

JAMES CLARENCE MANGAN

One of York Street's most famous residents was the poet and translator James Clarence Mangan, who lived at

No. 6 during the early 1820s. Wilmot Harrison, in *Memorable Dublin Houses*, records the artist W. F. Wakeman's description of Mangan:

> *There was … poor Clarence Mangan, with his queer puns and jokes, and odd little cloak and wonderful hat, which really resembled the tile that broomstick-riding witches are usually represented with, his flax-coloured wig, and false teeth.*[2]

Harrison also says that Mangan was made conspicuous by his huge pair of dark-green spectacles, and he would often be seen wandering around Dublin with an umbrella under each arm even if the weather was warm and sunny.

Mangan, born in 1803, was one of four children and the son of a poor shopkeeper, whom Mangan later blamed for all of his own failings. His father had originally been a schoolteacher from Limerick and in 1801 he married Catherine Smith, owner of a small grocery shop at Fishamble Street.

Mangan got his early education at a school in Saul's Court, where he is said to have studied the basics of Latin, French, Spanish and Italian. He became the family breadwinner at the age of fifteen after his father had been declared bankrupt for the eighth time, and began work as an apprentice at Kenrick's scrivener's office in York Street, where he worked for a number of years.

He took up writing around that time and contributed poetry, puzzles and other items to a variety of publications, including *The Comet*, a weekly satirical newspaper, and the *Dublin University Magazine*. In 1842 Mangan got a job as a clerk at the library in Trinity College and supplemented his small income by contributing articles to the *Nation* and the *Irish Penny Journal*.

By that time Mangan was drinking very heavily and one of his favourite haunts was the Bleeding Horse in Camden Street, which is still there today. He was also fond of smoking opium, but it is not clear if he was an addict. Mangan turned his hand to translations of Irish poetry, and *Dark Rosaleen*, Mangan's finest work, was published at that time.

In 1849 Ireland was devastated by a cholera epidemic and unfortunately Mangan contracted the deadly disease in May of that year. He was brought to a temporary hospital set up in Kilmainham known as 'the cholera sheds'. Mangan left 'the sheds' after a few days, however, and made his way to what would be his last home – a run-down garret in Bride Street.

Failing to recover, Mangan was taken to the Meath Hospital on 13 June and died there a week later. The poet knew that he was dying and spent his last days in the hospital scribbling notes on any scrap of paper that he could find. Unfortunately, his last writings were burned by an attendant immediately after his death, as she had been reprimanded earlier for not keeping the wards tidy.

Cholera victims were supposed to be buried immediately after death, but Mangan's funeral didn't take place until three days later. The cholera epidemic of 1849 had killed thousands and there weren't enough coffins or hearses to go round. Mangan was buried at Glasnevin cemetery on 23 June 1849 and the funeral was attended by only five of his closest friends.

CHARLES MATURIN

The author and clergyman Charles Robert Maturin lived at No. 37 York Street. Maturin, born in Dublin on 25 September 1782, is best known as the author of the best-selling Gothic classic *Melmoth the Wanderer*.

He came from a Dublin Huguenot family and attended Trinity College, from where he graduated in 1798. He became a minister in the Anglican Church and was appointed curate of St Peter's parish in Aungier Street in 1805. He first took up writing in order to supplement his miserable curate's income and his first three novels were published under the pseudonym of Denis Jasper Murphy. He also wrote a number of plays, the most successful of which, *Bertram*, enjoyed a long run at London's Drury Lane Theatre in 1816, despite receiving a savage review from Samuel Taylor Coleridge. The play's ultimate success brought in some extra money for Maturin and encouraged him to reveal his true identity.

Maturin's finest hour came with the publication of his Gothic masterpiece *Melmoth the Wanderer* in 1820. The novel – said to have been written by candlelight in Marsh's Library – is a tale of madness, alienation, paranoia and terror, and is considered by many to be the definitive Gothic novel. It is based on a fictional Irish landowner with Cromwellian roots called John Melmoth, who sells his soul to the devil in return for 150 years of life and prosperity.

The book was a huge literary success and has been translated into many languages. Literary giants, such as Balzac and Baudelaire, confessed to being influenced by Maturin's work. Maturin's York Street neighbour, James Clarence Mangan, was a big admirer of his work and Oscar Wilde adopted the nickname of Sebastian Melmoth after he was released from Reading Gaol.

However, despite the book's success, Maturin was still beset by financial difficulties. He and his wife, Henrietta Kingsbury, bought a large house at No. 37 York Street with the intention of turning it into a school. The venture was not a success, however, and they were forced to abandon the project due to their inability to attract a sufficient number of pupils to the school.

Maturin was known to have many unusual habits. His York Street neighbour Mangan once described seeing

Maturin strolling along the street dressed in a rug, with a shoe on one foot and a boot on the other. At other times he was spotted wandering the streets of Dublin wearing only a dressing gown and slippers.

While working on his novels, Maturin stuck a red wafer to his forehead as a warning to family and friends that he was not to be disturbed. He was also known to seal his lips shut with a sticky paste made from flour and water so that he wouldn't be tempted to talk to anyone while he was writing.

Maturin is perhaps best summed up in this passage written about him in the *Dublin University Magazine* in 1858:

> *He was eccentric in his habits, almost to insanity, and compounded of opposites; an inveterate reader of novels, an elegant preacher, an incessant dancer ... a coxcomb in dress and manner, an extensive reader, and vain of his person and reputation ...*[3]

Charles Maturin died on 30 October 1824 at the age of forty-two, following a short illness. He had suffered periodic bouts of ill health during his last years and it has been said that he died following an accidental overdose at his home on York Street.

***

Despite once being one of Dublin's most fashionable streets, over the latter half of the nineteenth century and early twentieth century York Street fell far from its prime, the majority of the houses becoming slums and tenement dwellings. Most of these have since been demolished, however, and nowadays York Street is dominated by medical facilities associated with the Royal College of Surgeons.

ROYAL COLLEGE
OF SURGEONS

The Royal College of Surgeons (RCSI) on Stephen's Green west, just along from the Stephen's Green Shopping Centre, first opened its doors to the public in 1810, though it was not the first building to be inhabited by the surgeons of Dublin. During the latter part of the seventeenth century, the Dublin Society of Surgeons used to meet every Thursday night at the Elephant tavern in Essex Street – that is, until it was burned down in 1681.

The Royal College of Surgeons on Stephen's Green west.

The surgeons had yet to receive their royal charter by this point. This meant that Dublin surgeons belonged to the same medieval guild as barbers, wig makers and apothecaries. Many of the upwardly mobile members of the medical profession weren't too happy being lumped in with the hairdressing fraternity and these other 'lower' professions. It is clear that the surgeons were attempting to divorce themselves from them as early as the beginning of the eighteenth century. In his *Account of the Schools of Surgery*, John Widdess quotes from an undated pamphlet that was written sometime around 1703. The pamphlet was titled *Reasons for Regulating the Practice of Surgery in the City of Dublin, by Making the Surgeons a distinct Society from the Barbers, Peruke-makers, etc. Humbly offered to the consideration of the Lords Spiritual and Temporal, and the Commons in Parliament assembled.* According to Widdess, the anonymous writer of the pamphlet complained that:

> *The present Corporation in this City is composed of Barbers, Surgeons, Apothecaries and Peruke-makers, which (instead of encouraging the true Professors of Surgery) is a refuge for Empiricks, Impudent Quacks, Women and other Idle Persons, who quit the trades to which they were bred, and wherein they might be useful to the Commonwealth, to undertake a Profession whereof they are entirely ignorant to the ruin of their Fellow Subjects. There is not any person (tho of the most*

infamous character) who cannot obtain his freedom of the
corporation, by vertue whereof the meanest Brother assumeth
of the Liberty, and it is a sufficient Recommendation for
him to Practice Surgery with as much authority as the most
Experienced Surgeon. There are in the Corporation at least
ten Barbers for one Surgeon so that it is impossible for the
Surgeons to make any Regulation because they must inevitably
be outvoted by the majority of the others.[4]

The surgeons finally got their way in 1784, when they received their royal charter from George III.

Despite the charter, the surgeons initially had some difficulty in obtaining suitable premises in which to practise. Dissections were instead carried out in individual surgeons' houses, but this stop-gap solution went nowhere near to fulfilling the demand. Numerous representations were made to the Irish parliament for funds, but to no avail.

The situation came to a head in 1788 when one of the high sheriffs of Dublin applied to the college to take in the body of a hanged criminal, Frederick Lambert, for dissection under the rules of the Chalking Act provided by parliament.

In response to the demand from Sheriff Tweedy, the secretary of the College of Surgeons replied:

I am to acquaint you that the College regret that it is not in their power to comply with the Act, by receiving the body, as Government has not yet enabled them to procure an Hall for Publick Dissection.[5]

Lambert's case is an interesting one. He was a notorious Dublin criminal whose exploits were recorded in the famous old Dublin street ballad 'The Night Before Larry was Stretched'. Lambert, who had been convicted of robbery in 1783, was not typical of the Dublin criminal fraternity, as he came from a wealthy family: his father was a lawyer and his brother owned several valuable properties around the city.

Lambert was initially sentenced to death, but was pardoned on the condition that he would leave Ireland for fourteen years. He initially agreed to those conditions and left the country, but returned just three years later. Shortly after his return, he was arrested and incarcerated in Newgate Prison, where he was held on remand until June 1788. Because of his family connections, Lambert was pardoned again, but this time the judge sentenced him to be transported to one of the colonies for the remainder of his life.

While he was awaiting transportation, however, he got into a fight with Francis Bathhurst, a violent criminal who was serving a sentence for throwing a three-year-old boy from a third-storey window. Lambert slashed Bathhurst with a razor and was about to finish him off when he was overpowered by other inmates.

Lambert was charged with assault under the Chalking Act, which allowed for the execution and dissection of criminals within two days of sentencing, was found guilty and was sentenced to death. The death sentence was carried out on 30 October 1788 in front of a vast crowd outside Newgate Prison. But the execution didn't go smoothly. The hangman used the wrong size of rope and Lambert was seen to struggle for several minutes before he died.

As for the surgeons, their first premises was a former charity home used to house orphans from St Peter's parish. This was in nearby Mercer Street. A house next door was also secured in order that the surgeons might have better access to the infamous Goat Alley (now Digges Lane) where the graverobbing inhabitants could supply a steady source of fresh cadavers for the surgeons' dissecting room with the minimum of fuss.

By the beginning of the nineteenth century, because of the Napoleonic wars, there was a huge increase in demand for surgeons in the army and the navy. Indeed, many in Dublin credited Napoleon with being one of the main reasons for the success of the new medical school. 'If one were asked to name two men to whom the College owed its early prosperity, one would be Napoleon Bonaparte ...'[6]

The surgeons needed a bigger premises to fulfil the demand and so the former Quaker burial ground at York Street, right in front of the main gateway to Stephen's Green, was purchased. The cemetery had not been used since the end of the seventeenth century when the Quakers opened a new burial ground in Cork Street. The Quakers sold the land to the College of Surgeons with the proviso that no bodies were to be dug up from the graveyard for 100 years on pain of a £2,000 fine, and that agreement was – apart from a few minor transgressions – adhered to until 1875 when further expansion took place on the site. Human remains found at that time were removed to other Quaker cemeteries in the city such as Cork Street or Temple Hill in Blackrock.

Building work under the direction of the architect Edward Parke began on the new premises at York Street in 1806 and was complete by 1810. A few years later it was described as being: 'extremely well-built, the basement storey being of mountain granite, and the superstructure of Portland-stone; the facade is simply elegant, and ornamented with six columns of the Doric order'.[7]

The new premises was described in *The Lancet* as:

> *a neat little structure which suddenly arose upon the scite of the quaker's burial ground, at the corner of York Street, Steven's Green. On the 17th March, 1806, the usual ceremony of laying*

the first stone was performed by the Lord Lieutenant, and as it now stands it reminds one very strongly of the appearance of these people, whose relics it has sacrilegiously supplanted, it looks for all the world like the genius of Quakerism personified in stone. Solid and substantial, no gew-gaw of the sculptor's art disfigures the simplicity of its style. With a facade of six pillars of Portland stone resting upon a basement of mountain granite, and supporting a cornice terminating in an angle at the top, stands the pride of the Irish surgery, and the terror of many a candidate, whose fate often depends upon its decrees.[8]

Obviously, as this was a college for training surgeons, the dissection of human bodies was a huge part of the students' lives. Even during the construction of the college, plans for the number of dissection theatres had to be revised upwards, and by 1812 more extensive dissecting rooms had to be built to cater for the increasing amount of students.

Warburton, Whitelaw and Walsh's *History of Dublin*, published in 1818, gives the following description of these 'Theatres of Anatomy':

The theatre in which the lectures are delivered is capable of accommodating between 300 and 400 students, besides what the gallery may contain, which is opened for the public during the dissection of malefactors. Adjoining the theatre are the professors' dissecting room, and two museums ... the dissecting

rooms are very commodious, and were added but lately to
the building … The public dissecting room is furnished with
twenty tables, at each of which two students are placed. There
is moreover, adjoining, a theatre for demonstration, which may
contain upwards of 100 spectators.[9]

BODYSNATCHERS

It seems obvious, but for the anatomists to practise their
trade, they needed a steady supply of bodies. Before 1832,
when the Anatomy Act was passed, the only way for a
trainee surgeon to obtain a cadaver legally was when the
body of an executed murderer was delivered to them.

This went no way near enough to meeting the demand
for bodies, so students had to source their own corpses on
which to practise. As a consequence, they turned to the
city's graverobbers, or 'sack-em-ups' as they were better
known in Dublin. There was a large number of graveyards
around Dublin, many of them isolated, providing easy
pickings for the resurrection men.

On occasion, some of the bodysnatchers who inhabited the lanes and alleyways behind the college didn't
even wait for the corpse to be laid in the ground. In late
December 1831, a gang of resurrectionists rushed into
a house in Bow Lane where a woman named O'Carroll
was being waked by her family and friends. Before anyone could stop them, the gang snatched the poor woman's

corpse and made off with it, dragging it through the filth and mud of the streets of Dublin in her grave clothes. The police were informed and they immediately went to the College of Surgeons to search for the body. Staff at the college told the police that they hadn't got it, but refused to give them permission to search the premises. It was said at the time that some of the city's most notorious grave-robbers were involved in the incident.[10]

Staff from the top down at the Royal College of Surgeons fully endorsed these activities. Widdess mentions that the professors of the college were expected to 'undertake the direction of the resurrection parties'.[11]

A number of the college porters carried on a lucrative sideline in the bodysnatching trade. The first of these was Anthony McMahon, who sold bodies to the students. He was succeeded by Neil Lawlor in 1805. However, it was said that Lawlor wasn't great at the resurrection game and was replaced a year later.

The best known of them was Christopher 'Kit' Dixon, who was a porter there until 1849. Another porter, Luke Redmond, was killed by an angry mob during a riot in 1828 as he was suspected of exporting bodies abroad. An inquiry established at the college to investigate Redmond's death and the practice of bodysnatching found that, while there was no evidence to implicate any of the professors in the murder, there was sufficient evidence that the College of Surgeons had been used as a holding place for bodies until they could be sold abroad. The committee was mainly concerned with the bad publicity surrounding this. After all, the practice of buying corpses from the resurrectionists had been going on for years with the tacit approval of the college authorities.

A man named Collins from nearby Peter Street and a man named Rae (also spelled Wray) from D'Olier Street were implicated as being the ringleaders of the scheme. Rae, who lived in Sandymount and was known to students as Doctor Rae, was identified as being the main man when it came to the exporting of bodies abroad. He would ship the bodies overseas labelled as pianos.

Another man heavily implicated in the scheme was the head porter Christopher 'Kit' Dixon, but he was not dismissed as it was felt that he had too much information on other staff members at the college. Despite the fact that at the inquiry Dixon was said to have 'scandalously violated the truth in every particular', he remained on in his position at the college for another twenty-one years, until he retired in 1849.[12]

The vexed problem of obtaining a legal supply of bodies to practise on ended in 1832 with the advent of the Ana-tomy Act, which provided bodies from workhouses and hospitals for the surgeons. The sack-em-ups were no more.

***

The college went from strength to strength during the nineteenth century and several RCSI graduates were responsible for introducing innovative practices in the field of Irish medicine. RCSI member and professor of anatomy John McDonnell, for example, performed the first operation under anaesthetic at the Richmond Hospital in 1847. Another graduate, Robert McDonnell, performed the first blood transfusion in Ireland at Jervis Street Hospital in 1865. The first women were admitted to the college in 1885, and the following year Mary Dawson became its first licentiate. Six years later, in 1891, Emily Winifred Dickson became the first female fellow at the RCSI.

The college saw some action during the 1916 Rising when it was briefly occupied by the Irish Citizen Army under the command of Michael Mallin and Countess Markievicz. Both were subsequently sentenced to death for their roles in the rebellion. Mallin was executed by firing squad in Kilmainham Gaol, while Markievicz was ultimately reprieved. Even today the college bears scars of the battle, with some bullet holes still marking the front of the building.

Today, the RCSI employs over 1,000 staff and its schools of medicine, pharmacy, physiotherapy and nursing cater to 4,000 medical students from all around the world.

UNITARIAN CHURCH

The Unitarian Church on St Stephen's Green west was built in 1863 and it boasts some fine examples of stained glass. Work on the main window of the church was carried out by the artist Sarah Purser, who was the first female member of the Royal Hibernian Academy. The Unitarians, who originally came from Bristol, first came to Ireland in 1673. They had a meeting house in Wood Street, and then, in 1763, moved to another premises in Strand Street.

Attached to the church is Damer Hall, which today hosts all sorts of interesting gatherings. During the 1950s Damer Hall hosted a 200-seater Irish language theatre called *Amharclann An Damer* (Damer Thea-

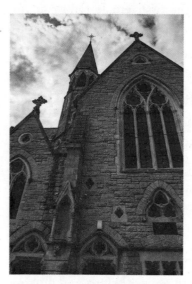

The Unitarian Church at Stephen's Green contains some fine examples of stained glass.

tre) and it came to prominence in 1957 when it hosted the world premiere of Brendan Behan's classic play *The Hostage.*

Damer Hall is named in honour of one of its patrons, Joseph Damer, a former Cromwellian soldier who came to Dublin in 1662. Damer was a wealthy young man and he founded what was to become a very lucrative and profitable banking and money-lending business from a room in the London Tavern in Fishamble Street.

Damer's financial wheeling and dealing soon brought him to the attention of Dean Jonathan Swift, who wasn't too fond of bankers and moneylenders. He particularly despised Damer, and when the latter died in 1720, Swift and his friend Thomas Sheridan composed an elegy to him:

> *He walked the streets and wore a threadbare cloak;*
> *He dined and supped at charge of other folk;*
> *And by his looks, had he held out his palms;*
> *He might be thought an object fit for alms*
> *Oh! London Tavern, thou hast lost a friend,*
> *Though in thy walls he ne'er did farthing spend.*[13]

Not everyone in Dublin held the same view of Damer as Swift, however. The following obituary appeared in *Whalley's Newsletter* on 11 July 1720:

On Wednesday last Mr. Joseph Deamer [sic] died at his house in Smithfield upwards of ninety years of age, with not above £340,000, and last night was interred in St Paul's church in Oxmantown Green attended by a numerous train of gentlemen's as well as by hackney coaches ... I knew him upwards of fifty years, and though his fortune was all his own acquiring I believe that it was every penny got honestly. His purse was open to all he believed to be honest or where he thought his money secure ...

Damer had the reputation of being a miser, but after his death it emerged that he had donated large sums of money to worthy causes during his lifetime and funded several charities throughout Dublin. One of these was a charity school attached to the Unitarian Church of which he was a member. This establishment was named the Damer School in his honour and it continued to receive funding from his estate until well into the twentieth century.

Damer also established a house of refuge on Parnell Street for destitute widows. The house provided shelter for twenty widows, housing them in their own private rooms, and provided them with a weekly allowance of food, fuel and a nominal sum of spending money.

The proprietor of the above-named *Whalley's Newsletter*, John Whalley, was actually a neighbour of Damer and was one of the early residents on the west side of the Green. He lived there at the sign of 'The Blew Posts', next door to

'The Wheel of Fortune', from 1691 until 1698. Whalley was an astrologer, publisher of newspapers and almanacs and a quack doctor. He was famous for his almanacs, the best-known of which was *Dr Whalley's Almanac*.

Whalley was a rabid anti-Catholic and he was once forced to stand in the pillory at the Tholsel, where he was pelted with rotten eggs and vegetables, for his anti-Catholic rantings, tirades against the pope and support for William of Orange in 1688. At another time he called for the castration of Catholic priests and for the destruction of Catholic books.

Around that time, Whalley became the target of what was known as one of the bitterest satires ever composed, when the Gaelic poet Ferdoragh O'Daly wrote a twenty-one verse poem about him after Whalley had O'Daly's brother prosecuted and hanged. In the poem, Ferdoragh alleged that Whalley had been a devil worshipper, had caused crops to wither and had destroyed young animals in the womb:

> *He then commences to wither the astrologer with imprecations, prays that various violent diseases may attack him, and calls down upon Whalley the curses of God, the angels, the saints, and of all good men.*[14]

Whalley died in 1724 and the following verse, taken from

an elegy written by Jonathan Swift, is generally believed to have been composed for him:

> *Here five foot deep, lies on his back*
> *A cobbler, starmonger and Quack*
> *Who to the stars in pure good will*
> *Does his best to look upward still*
> *Weep all ye customers who use*
> *His pills, his almanacs and shoes.*[15]

In June 1942 a letter published in *The Irish Times* asserted that the first public shooting of a film in Dublin took place beside the Unitarian Church in 1897. According to the unnamed correspondent, the scene depicted a rescue from the upper floor of one of the houses. Smoke billowed from the windows and a frantically waving man was duly rescued by a helmeted fireman from the Dublin fire brigade. The correspondent says the fire engine came from nearby Chatham Street and that:

> *On the street below a second camera-man was busily 'closing up' all the paraphernalia of fire-fighting – the engine, the hose-rolling, the hydrants, etc. Presently he turned his lens and handle upon two apparently inebriated gentlemen, who, after the manner of circus clowns, burlesqued the part of civilian helpers, being finally dowsed for their pains by the brigade hoses.*[16]

Nowadays, the Unitarian Church on St Stephen's Green – though rooted in Presbyterianism – has instead put an emphasis on personal faith, with congregation members being allowed to pick the readings and musical interludes during their service.

MERCER
STREET

MARY MERCER/MERCER'S HOSPITAL

On Tuesday 4 March 1735 a wealthy spinster, Mary Mercer of Great Ship Street, died, leaving a fortune of £6,000 to be used to aid the poor of Dublin. Half of the money was to be used to set up a charity school for impoverished and destitute young girls, and the rest was to go to helping the sick and poor of four inner-city parishes.

Mary's father, George Mercer, an Englishman, came to Dublin in 1663 and was admitted to Trinity College as a 'pensioner' (a fee-paying student). He became a fellow of Trinity in 1670 and obtained his medical degree ten years later. At that time fellows were forbidden by college rules to marry – being a fellow in those days was basically seen as being effectively married to the college – but Mercer flouted this rule when he met and married a woman named Mary Barry.

Fellows did actually get married, but it was usually done discreetly and the wives were passed off with a nudge and a wink as the fellow's sister. However, Archbishop Marsh, founder of Marsh's Library, somehow got wind of Mercer's arrangement and poor old Mercer was sacked from his post as vice-provost of Trinity. Not long after this humiliation, he died, at the relatively young age of forty-two.

George's daughter clearly had a deep interest in helping the poor of Dublin. In 1724, for example, Mary Mercer built a house 'containing four rooms, to be employed for the habitation and reception of twenty poor girls or such other poor persons as she should from time to time direct and appoint to live therein' on the site of the old St Stephen's leper hospital at Stephen Street.

Mercer decided to move this school to a rural area in 1734, far from the temptations of the city, obtaining lands at Rathcoole for that purpose. She handed over the school building at Stephen Street to the trustees of St Peter's parish on the condition that it be used for the care of 'poor sick and diseased persons' and those suffering from 'the falling sickness, lunacy, leprosy and the like ...'[17]

Mercer's Hospital first opened its doors to the Dublin public in 1734 with the help of a grant of £50 from the corporation of Dublin. There were only ten beds in the hospital at that time and the doctors and surgeons gave their services free of charge. The city's apothecaries also helped out with contributions of free medicine. By 1738 the number of beds had increased to sixty and an extension containing a sweathouse and bathing facilities was added on.

Mercer's Hospital closed in 1983, having given 250 years of service to the Dublin public, all stemming from Mary Mercer's generosity and altruism. The building – apart from the façade – was demolished in 1989, but her name lives on through the street that is named in her honour.

Mercer's Medical Centre on the site of Mary Mercer's old hospital for Dublin's sick and poor.

MERCER
STREET UPPER

Located between Cuffe Street and York Street, it was originally called Love Lane, a name that lasted until 1733, when it was renamed Little Cuffe Street. The name changed again to French Street in 1776, which lasted until 1860, when the street was given its present name of Mercer Street Upper. However, the change of name from French Street in 1860 did little – in the short term, at least – to rehabilitate the street's reputation as a den of iniquity.

Prostitution was rampant in the area at that time and as J. V. O'Brien, in his book *Dear Dirty Dublin*, noted: 'the upper class of prostitute played host to Dublin's officers and gentlemen in French Street and Clarendon Street without interference from the law'. He also claimed, citing 'contemporary sources', that '1500 well-known prostitutes' were choking Grafton Street at that time.[18]

In a government report in 1882, Rawton McNamara of the Westmoreland Lock Hospital commented on the notoriety of French Street and the surrounding area. 'Almost all the houses of ill fame were in a street called French Street, and another street called Clarendon Street.

French Street is very close to the square in which I live ... St Stephen's Green Park and we did not like to have such people near us.'[19]

The street was full of larger-than-life characters, including the well-known Dublin madam Fanny Stuart. On Monday 19 September 1853 large crowds gathered outside No. 24 French Street, where she ran a brothel or a 'house of bad repute' as it was described in *The Freeman's Journal*. The reason for the excitement was that, on the previous night, a young prostitute named Emma Fawcett had been shot and seriously injured by one of her customers, the perpetrator then taking his own life.

The dead man was initially named as Robert James Webster, who had stayed at Fanny Stuart's establishment for some weeks prior to the incident. Webster had described himself as Queen Victoria's veterinary surgeon and said that he was in Dublin to look after the queen's horses. During his short time in the city, Webster, who had a Scottish accent, had been involved in a number of violent incidents including one where he had fired a pistol at a well-known beggar named Buckley who plied his trade at Knockmaroon Gate in the Phoenix Park. On another occasion, he attacked one of the other clients at Fanny Stuart's with a knife and only stopped when Emma Fawcett threatened him with a poker. Webster was a heavy drinker and money seemed to be no object to him. He lavished money and drink on Emma and the other French Street ladies and bought them presents.

After the subsequent inquest into his death, 'Webster' was taken to Mount Jerome cemetery where he was laid to rest. Bizarrely, it wasn't eternal rest, because the body of the unfortunate man was to be dug up three times in the next fortnight. Webster's remains were first exhumed a week after his death at the request of a Mrs Forbes from London, who thought that the description circulated in the British press resembled that of her missing son. Mrs Forbes didn't recognise the corpse, so the remains were reburied, only to be dug up a few days later when Mrs Forbes' other son arrived from London and asked to see the dead man's remains. He was joined in viewing the corpse by a woman named Anne Roose from Nottingham, who thought it might be her brother. Despite the fact that rapid decomposition had set in, both Forbes and Roose were certain that the man in the coffin was not their relative.

The remains were buried for a third time and that seemed to be the end of the matter until a director of the Jedburgh Bank in Scotland arrived in Dublin and asked to see the dead man's remains. Incredibly, the corpse was exhumed again and this time it was positively identified as Inverness native James McFarlane. McFarlane had been a clerk at a Jedburgh wool merchants and had been charged on 25 August of that year with embezzling the bank to the tune of £700, after which he fled to Dublin.

The bad publicity of this scandal obviously wasn't enough to deter Fanny. Two years later she was summoned to appear in a Dublin court for refusing to let a policeman search her French Street premises under the tippling act (designed to prevent the drinking of alcohol on unlicensed premises). In court, Fanny's legal representative accused the policeman, Sergeant Fitzpatrick, of trying to drive her and other French Street madams out of the area. Her barrister, Charles Fitzgerald, also criticised the behaviour of the police in general, saying that they 'abused their authority, and that they were indirectly endeavouring, under the pretence of preventing the sale of drink, to scatter the females living in those houses, throughout the city'.[20]

Sergeant Fitzpatrick refused to answer the accusations, saying that he was acting on instructions from a 'higher authority'. Judge Bourke fined Fanny ten shillings and commented that while he saw that prostitution was a nuisance in Dublin, the problem would get much worse if the women were allowed to move into 'respectable localities' of the city. He also revealed that a 'gentleman' had approached him a few days earlier to help him get rid of two prostitutes from his lodging house after they had been hounded out of French Street.[21]

Sergeant Fitzpatrick and his ilk ultimately got their way, however. Rawton McNamara explained how the French Street brothels were eventually broken up when the Dublin authorities made a concerted effort to shut them down. Policemen stood outside the doors of the brothels over a period of weeks, taking down the particulars of everyone who entered them. This quickly had the effect of forcing the madams out of the area – though it didn't put them out of business. All that happened was that the red-light district moved across the Liffey to an area around Mecklenburgh Street and Montgomery Street. This, in time, became the infamous Monto, soon to be known as 'the worst sink of iniquity in the British Isles'.[22]

Nowadays, Mercer Street Upper is a much tamer place, being mainly a residential area.

GOAT ALLEY/ DIGGES LANE

Not far from French Street was another den of iniquity: Goat Alley. Even by Dublin standards, Goat Alley was a dark and dangerous place during the eighteenth and nineteenth centuries. In the summer of 1764, for example, a man was placed in the pillory and whipped from Newgate Prison to College Green after he had been found guilty of assaulting a young girl in Goat Alley.[23]

The place had such a bad reputation at that time that even the officers of the parish watch wouldn't patrol there. In April 1773 it was reported in the *Hibernian Journal* that the 'Watch do not stand at the corner of Goat Alley and Little Longford Street, as is necessary in so dangerous a neighbourhood.'[24]

Because of its bad reputation, Goat Alley was renamed as Digges Lane by the city authorities in 1784. However, despite the change, many newspapers and publications still referred to it as Goat Alley right up until the 1830s.

The change of name also didn't help improve the area. In 1835, a resident of Digges Lane complained about the high number of brothels operating in the area. John

Bramble said that he had lived in Digges Lane for fifteen years and that there had been brothels there during and before that time. He described the whole area as 'a second Gomorrah'.[25] Bramble also complained of an increasing number 'of those miserable outcasts and their companions, robbers and resurrection men' living in the area. [26]

The working women of Digges Lane could spot an easy mark from a mile away. Take the case of the hapless Tom Quinn, described in *Saunders's News-Letter* on 2 October 1830 as a 'gallant gay Lothario' from Co. Wicklow who had travelled to Dublin for a civic event at the Mansion House in Dawson Street. Afterwards, Tom did a bit of sightseeing around Dublin and later on, feeling a bit hungry, he retired to a tavern in Fleet Street where he treated himself to a dinner of chicken and ham and washed it down with half a dozen glasses of punch.

Well fortified, Tom left the tavern and, as was reported in *Saunders's News-Letter*, he had stopped to admire 'the national bit of architecture', the Parliament House (now the Bank of Ireland) in College Green, when he was accosted by 'another bit of architecture, which presented itself in the shape of a dashing looking woman who asked him to escort her home'.

Tom readily agreed and accompanied her back to a lodging house in Goat Alley where he spent the night with her. When he woke in the morning, poor Tom found that he'd been relieved of the princely sum of £7 10s, a small fortune back in those days. However, the story had a happy ending for Tom on this occasion. When apprehended by a police officer by the name of Mackey, the woman still had all of Tom's money in her possession. The money was returned to him and she was sent to Newgate Prison.[27]

The same police officer was obviously well versed when it came to dealing with the residents of Goat Alley. Two years earlier, in December 1828, Officer Mackey managed to retrieve the property of 'a gentleman whose name is unknown' from a Goat Alley prostitute named Fanny Conroy.[28] Fanny had stolen £40 from the man while he was asleep and Mackey arrested her in Crane Street with the remaining £24 of the man's money.

Some fifty years earlier, another Wicklow man had a similar experience in Goat Alley. The Dublin newspapers reported that a grazier was robbed of 11 guineas by a prostitute and her accomplices at a house of ill fame in Goat Alley. Two men attacked the grazier, beat him severely and ran off with his money.[29]

In his book *Evenings in the Duffrey* published in 1869, the folklorist Patrick Kennedy recounted a tale of advice given to a friend, warning him to stay clear of Goat Alley:

> *But after all, the only real danger won't be near until you get to the city. So if you have any valuable thing to carry from Luke*

Byrne's, of Francis Street, down towards Stephen's Green or the
Bank, take a couple of men with you out of Luke's house, and
let one go before, and the other behind. Keep your parcel tightly
tucked up under your left arm, and a pistol cocked in the right
hand ... Keep a sharp look out at the corners of Hanover Lane,
Drury Lane, and Goat Alley, and when you find yourself safe
as far as William Street or Stephen's Green, you may put your
pistol up ...[30]

Goat Alley wasn't just a centre for brothels and pickpockets; it was also home to some of Dublin's most
prolific graverobbers. One of these was Michael Farrell.
In an article headed 'Sacrilegious Spoliation of the
Dead', Farrell was named as one of the perpetrators of
the removal of the corpse of a thirteen-year-old girl from
Aungier Street church:

On Tuesday, a man named Michael Farrell, a well known
resurrectionist, was arrested in Goat Alley, charged with being
one of the principals in the removal of Miss Dougherty [sic]
from the vaults of White friar Street Chapel. An investigation
into this extraordinary affair will take place tomorrow.[31]

Thirteen-year-old Margaret Dogherty had been buried
in a vault at the church on Aungier Street on 15 March
1831 and her remains were stolen the following day. By

the time the child's distraught father, Theobald Dogherty, recovered the child's remains, all of her hair had been shaved off and presumably sold, while all of her teeth had been removed and probably sold to the dentists of Dublin. A golden, heart-shaped locket that had been buried with the girl was also missing.

The clerk of the chapel, John Prenter, gave evidence that Margaret had been buried in the aisle of the church encased in brick under clay and two layers of flagstones. Her understandably devastated father told the court that he had laid his daughter in the coffin himself and it was he that found her in the anatomy house at Trinity College. A porter at Trinity College gave evidence that Michael Farrell, along with two accomplices named Kit Carney and James McClean, had left the girl's body at the anatomy house there early on the morning of 16 March.

Farrell was found guilty of the crime and sentenced to a year's imprisonment at the Richmond Bridewell.[32]

Terrible things happened in Goat Alley all the time, but perhaps the worst incident in the alley's history occurred on Monday 21 February 1831. The city awoke that morning to the awful news that two children had been murdered by their own father. The man, named Lynch, had been a watchman, but he was sacked from his job after he was found in a brothel in Goat Alley. Lynch killed the two children aged four and nine months, and then cut his own throat.[33]

Later that year a man named Michael Donnelly was jailed after making several attempts to take his own life. He had been cut down from a tree in the Phoenix Park on one occasion and he was apprehended with a rope in his pocket soon afterwards. At his trial, Donnelly's wife told the court that her husband had been in the habit of spending his pension on 'the infamous inhabitants of Goat Alley and returned destitute of clothing to his family'.[34]

Another notorious resident of Goat Alley was Elizabeth Hannigan, who was better known as 'Mad Bet'. Bet, who was blind, appeared on a vagrancy charge in a Dublin court in July 1836, where a city watchman named Owen Rafferty gave evidence that he knew Bet as a dreadful character who exposed herself in the streets 'in a most disgusting manner'. He also said in court that if people didn't give Bet what she asked for she would break their windows.[35]

CONCLUSION

Many of the places mentioned in this book no longer exist. Streets and alleyways in close proximity to St Stephen's Green, such as that 'sink of sin' and home to pimps, prostitutes, thieves and pickpockets, Goat Alley, is long gone. In the same vein, French Street, once one of Dublin's most notorious red-light districts, was cleared out in the late eighteenth century and renamed because of its less-than-salubrious reputation. At the other end of the scale, Peg Plunkett's high-class brothel just off Grafton Street, which was particularly beloved of politicians, bankers and the lord lieutenant of Ireland, suffered a similar fate. No trace of it remains today.

While many of the characters in the book – revolutionaries, poets, novelists and politicians – who inhabited the big houses on Stephen's Green itself and the surrounding streets are remembered with plaques, memorials and statues, no such memorial exists for the many hundreds hanged at the Green down through the centuries, some of whose stories are included here. There's nothing left now at the crossroads of Baggot Street and Fitzwilliam Street to remind us that this was once very much part of St Stephen's Green, or to alert us to the fact that it used to be the killing fields of Dublin; the place where many went to their deaths at the end of a hangman's rope.

All of the stories recorded here afford only a brief glimpse of the darker side of this small area of Dublin's history, but I hope that the reader has found them as interesting and as illuminating to read as I did in researching them.

ENDNOTES

INTRODUCTION

1   *The Freeman's Journal*, 25 January 1821.
2   McCready, C. T., *Dublin Street Names, Dated and Explained* (Hodges Figgis & Co., Dublin, 1892), p. 39.

ST STEPHEN'S GREEN

1   Gilbert, J. T., *Calendar of Ancient Records of Dublin*, Vol. I (Joseph Dollard, Dublin, 1889), p. 81.
2   *Ibid.*, p. 159.
3   *Ibid.*, p. 253.
4   Gilbert, *Calendar of Ancient Records of Dublin*, Vol. IV, pp. 256–7.
5   *Ibid.*, p. 383.
6   *Hibernian Journal*, 26 February 1773.
7   *Ibid.*, 2 November 1781.
8   *Ibid.*, 7 June 1783.
9   *Dublin Intelligence*, 18 December 1711.
10 O'Reilly, Andrew, *Reminiscences of an Emigrant Milesian* (R. Bentley, London, 1853), pp. 151–2.
11 Le Fanu, Joseph Sheridan, *The Cock and Anchor* (William Curry, Dublin, 1845), pp. 326–8.
12 *The Irish Times*, 24 October 1927.
13 *The Freeman's Journal*, 31 January 1764.
14 *Pue's Occurrences*, 25 September 1756.
15 Clarke, D., *Dublin* (B. T. Batsford, London, 1977), p. 63.
16 Collins, J., *Life in Old Dublin* (J. Duffy, Dublin, 1913), p.147.
17 King, J. and Joly, J. R., *The case of John Atherton, Bishop of Waterford in Ireland* (Luke Stokoe, London, 1710), p. 9.
18 *Ibid.*, p. 11.
19 Bernard, N., *The political ballance, for 1754* (Roger Lapis, London, 1754), p. 36.

20 *Ibid.*, p. 38.
21 Bernard, N., *Some memorials of the life and penitent death of Dr John Atherton, Bishop of Waterford in Ireland who was executed in Dublin* (London, 1711)
22 Kelly, J., *Gallows Speeches from Eighteenth-Century Ireland* (Four Courts Press, Dublin, 2001), p. 130.
23 *Ibid.*
24 *Ibid.*, p. 132.
25 *Derby Mercury*, 27 June 1727.
26 *Ipswich Journal*, 7 June 1735.
27 *Dublin Courant*, 29 December 1747.
28 *The Freeman's Journal*, 10 August 1775.
29 *Saunders's News-Letter*, 9 February 1778.
30 *Dublin Evening Post*, 17 November 1781.
31 Porter, F. T., *Twenty Years' Recollections' of an Irish Police Magistrate* (Hodges, Foster & Figgis, Dublin, 1880), p. 4.
32 *Saunders's News-Letter*, 16 August 1782.
33 *Ibid.*, 23 December 1782.
34 *Hibernian Journal*, 23 December 1782.
35 *Ibid.*, 17 December 1783.
36 *Saunders's News-Letter*, 21 July 1784.
37 *Hibernian Journal*, 23 August 1784.
38 *Ibid.*
39 Anon., *A further and more perticular account of the cruel desperate and bloody fight and uproar, that happen'd in Ireland on Monday the 6th of May 1700, between the weavers and butchers* (London, 1700).
40 *Ibid.*
41 *Dublin Intelligence*, 11 June 1726.
42 *Ibid.*
43 *Ibid.*
44 *The Irish Times*, 20 August 1907.
45 *The Freeman's Journal*, 20 August 1907.
46 *Irish Independent*, 24 November 1967.
47 *Ibid.*
48 *Sunday Independent*, 19 November 1967.
49 Sullivan, Timothy Daniel, *Speeches from the Dock* (M. H. Gill & Son, Dublin, 1953), p. 60.

50   Ward, M., *Hanna Sheehy Skeffington, Suffragette and Sinn Féiner: Her Memoirs and Political Writings* (UCD Press, Dublin, 2017), p. 68.

NORTH OF THE GREEN

1   Harrison, W., *Memorable Dublin Houses* (Leckie, Dublin, 1890), p. 41.
2   *Daily Express* (Dublin), 22 November 1937.
3   Harrison (1890), p. 53.
4   *Ibid.*
5   Craig, M., *Dublin 1660–1860: The Shaping of a City* (Liberties Press, Dublin, 2009), p. 135.
6   Moore, G., *Parnell and his Island* (Swan, Sonnenschein, Lowrey & Co., Dublin, 1887), pp. 31–3.
7   Gilbert, J. T., *A History of the City of Dublin*, Vol. III (Keeling & Shew, J. McGlashan and Gill, Dublin, 1859), p. 294.
8   Hemans, F., *The Poetical Works of Mrs. Felicia Hemans* (Phillips, Sampson & Co., Boston, 1849), p. 160.
9   Kevin O'Shiel, Bureau of Military History Witness Statement (hereafter BMH WS) 1770, p. 699.
10   *Ibid.*
11   *Ibid.*, p. 698.
12   Gilbert, *A History of the City of Dublin*, Vol. III, pp. 29–30.
13   *Ibid.*, pp. 204–5.
14   Lyons, Mary (ed.), *The Memoirs of Mrs. Leeson, Madam, 1727–1797* (The Lilliput Press, Dublin, 1995), p. 80.
15   *Ibid.*, p. 71.

SOUTH OF THE GREEN

1   Whaley, T. and Sullivan, E., *Buck Whaley's Memoirs* (De La More Press, London, 1906), p. 224.
2   *Ibid.*, p. 270.
3   *The Irish Times*, 13 July 1984.
4   *Ibid.*
5   *Ibid.*
6   *The Irish Press*, 9 August 1993.
7   *The Irish Times*, 28 July 1984.
8   Harrison (1890), p. 44.

9   *The Freeman's Journal*, 20 May 1837.

10   *Waterford Mail*, 17 July 1824.

11   *Daily Express* (Dublin), 29 July 1864.

12   *The Freeman's Journal*, 21 September 1872.

13   *Saunders's News-Letter*, 12 July 1777.

14   Fitzpatrick, W. J., *The Sham Squire and the Informers of 1798* (W. B. Kelly, Dublin, 1866), p. 195.

15   Gilbert, *A History of the City of Dublin*, Vol. III, p. 29.

16   *Ibid.*, pp. 29–30.

17   *Dublin Evening Post*, 13 August 1789.

18   Barrington, J., *Personal Sketches of his Own Times* (H. Colburn and R. Bentley, London, 1830), p. 314.

19   *The Freeman's Journal*, 25 January 1821.

20   *Ibid.*

21   *Ibid.*

22   *Ibid.*, 28 September 1822.

23   *Dublin Evening Post*, 8 March 1831.

24   *The Pilot*, 8 March 1831.

25   *Dublin Mercantile Advertiser*, 6 May 1833.

26   *Daily Express* (Dublin), 8 May 1878.

27   *The Freeman's Journal*, 8 May 1878.

28   Barrington, J., *The Ireland of Sir Jonah Barrington, Selections from his Personal Sketches* (Washington, 1967), p. 194.

29   *Ibid.*, p. 192.

30   Fitzpatrick, W. J., *Secret Service Under Pitt* (Longmans, Green & Co., New York, 1892), p. 195.

31   *The Irish Press*, 21 August 1963.

32   *Ibid.*

33   *Ibid.*

34   *The Irish Times*, 15 March 1997.

35   Burt, D. S., *The Novel 100: A Ranking of the Greatest Novels of All Time* (Checkmark Books, New York, 2004), p. 567.

EAST OF THE GREEN

1   *The Irish Times*, 2 July 2011.

2   *Ibid.*

3   *The Fitzwilliam Post*, 14 February 1987.

4   *Ibid.*

WEST OF THE GREEN

1   *The Freeman's Journal*, 9 July 1886.

2   Harrison (1890), pp. 30–1.

3   *Ibid.*, p. 32.

4   Widdess, J., *A Dublin School of Medicine and Surgery* (E. & S. Living-stone, Edinburgh, 1949), pp. 4–5.

5   *Ibid.*, p. 14.

6   *Ibid.*, p. 27.

7   Warburton, J., Whitelaw, J. and Walsh, R., *History of the City of Dublin*, Vol. II (W. Bulmer & Co., London, 1818), p. 753.

8   *The Lancet*, Vol. 1 (1823–4), p. 398.

9   *Ibid.*, pp. 751–2.

10   *The Drogheda Argus and Leinster Journal*, 31 December 1831.

11   Widdess (1949), p. 33.

12   *Ibid.*, pp. 33–5.

13   Sheridan, T., *The Poems of Thomas Sheridan*, ed. Robert Hogan (University of Delaware Press, New Jersey, 1994), pp. 106–8.

14   Gilbert, *A History of the City of Dublin*, Vol. I, p. 190.

15   *Ibid.*, p. 192.

16   *The Irish Times*, 23 June 1942.

17   *Irish Builder & Engineer*, 15 January 1897.

18   O'Brien, J. V., *Dear, Dirty Dublin: A City in Distress* (University of California Press, Berkeley, 1982), p.190.

19   *Great Britain. Parliament. House of Commons. (1882). Report from the select committee on contagious diseases acts: Together with the proceedings of the committee, minutes of evidence and appendix* (London, 1882), Q 6472.

20   *The Freeman's Journal*, 30 July 1855.

21   *Ibid.*

22   O'Brien (1982), p. 193.

23   *Dublin Courier*, 22 August 1764.

24   *Hibernian Journal*, 19 April 1773.

25   Luddy, M., *Prostitution and Irish Society 1800–1940* (Cambridge University Press, Cambridge, 2007), p. 22.

26   *Ibid.*

27 *Saunders's News-Letter*, 2 October 1830.

28 *Ibid.*, 1 January 1829.

29 *Ibid.*, 11 March 1779.

30 Kennedy, P., *Evenings in the Duffrey* (McGlashan & Gill, Dublin, 1875), p. 111.

31 *Dublin Morning Register*, 24 March 1831.

32 *Cork Constitution*, 12 April 1831.

33 *The Freeman's Journal*, 21 February 1831.

34 *The Pilot*, 15 August 1831.

35 *The Freeman's Journal*, 25 July 1836.

BIBLIOGRAPHY

PUBLISHED SOURCES

Anon., *A further and more perticular account of the cruel desperate and bloody fight and uproar, that happen'd in Ireland on Monday the 6th of May 1700, between the weavers and butchers. As also the great number of men that were wounded and kill'd on both sides, some having their heads, arms, backs, and leggs broke, in a cruel and terriable manner; with other dreadful circumstances that occasion'd it* (London, 1700)

Barrington, J., *Personal Sketches of his Own Times* (H. Colburn and R. Bentley, London, 1830)

Barrington, J., *The Ireland of Sir Jonah Barrington, Selections from his Personal Sketches* (Washington, 1967)

Bennett, D., *Encyclopaedia of Dublin* (Gill & Macmillan, Dublin, 2005)

Bernard, N., *Some memorials of the life and penitent death of Dr John Atherton, Bishop of Waterford in Ireland who was executed in Dublin* (London, 1711)

Bernard, N., *The political ballance, for 1754: The mock-patriot, for 1753. To which is added, the case of John Atherton, Bishop of Waterford in Ireland, who was convicted of beastiality with a cow and other creatures* (Roger Lapis, London, 1754)

Burt, D. S., *The Novel 100: A Ranking of the Greatest Novels of All Time* (Checkmark Books, New York, 2004)

Cameron, C. H., *History of the Royal College of Surgeons* (Fannin & Co., Dublin, 1910)

Clarke, D., *Dublin* (B. T. Batsford, London, 1977)

Coates, T. (ed.), *The Irish Uprising 1914–21* (Stationery Office Books, Norwich, 2000)

Collins, J., *Life in Old Dublin* (J. Duffy, Dublin, 1913)

Cosgrave, D., *North Dublin City and Environs* (Catholic Truth Society, Dublin, 1909)

Cowell, J., *Where They Lived in Dublin* (O'Brien Press, Dublin, 1980)

Craig, M., *Dublin 1660–1860: The Shaping of a City* (Liberties Press, Dublin, 2009)

D'Alton, J., *The History of the County Dublin* (Hodges and Smith, Dublin, 1838)

Dickson, D. (ed.), *The Gorgeous Mask: Dublin 1700–1850* (Trinity History Workshop, Dublin, 1987)

Fitzpatrick, W. J., *Lady Morgan: Her Career, Literary and Personal* (C. J. Skeet, London, 1860)

Fitzpatrick, W. J., *Memoirs of Richard Whately* (R. Bentley, London, 1864)

Fitzpatrick, W. J., *The Sham Squire and the Informers of 1798* (W. B. Kelly, Dublin, 1866)

Fitzpatrick, W. J., *Secret Service Under Pitt* (Longmans, Green & Co., New York, 1892)

Fleetwood, J., *The Irish Body Snatchers: A History of Body Snatching in Ireland* (Tomar Publications, Dublin, 1988)

Gilbert, J. T., *A History of the City of Dublin*, Vols I–III (Keeling & Shew, J. McGlashan and Gill, Dublin, 1859)

Gilbert, J. T. (ed.) and Gilbert, Lady, *Calendar of Ancient Records of Dublin*, Vols I–XIX (Joseph Dollard, Dublin, 1889–1944)

Haliday, C., *The Scandinavian Kingdom of Dublin* (Irish University Press, Shannon, 1969)

Harris, W., *History of the Antiquities of the City of Dublin* (Laurence Flinn and James Williams, Dublin, 1766)

Harrison, W., *Memorable Dublin Houses* (Leckie, Dublin, 1890)

Hemans, F., *The Poetical Works of Mrs. Felicia Hemans* (Phillips, Sampson & Co., Boston, 1849)

Henry, B., *Dublin Hanged: Crime, Law Enforcement and Punishment in Late Eighteenth-century Dublin* (Irish Academic Press, Dublin, 1994)

Hoare, Sir Richard, *Journal of a Tour in Ireland, A.D. 180* (W. Miller, London, 1807)

Igoe, V., *Dublin Burial Grounds and Graveyards* (Wolfhound Press, Dublin, 2001)

Joyce, Weston St. John, *The Neighbourhood of Dublin* (M. H. Gill & Son, Dublin, 1921)

Kelly, F., *A History of Kilmainham Gaol: The Dismal House of Little Ease* (Mercier Press, Cork, 1988)

Kelly, J., *Gallows Speeches from Eighteenth-Century Ireland* (Four Courts Press, Dublin, 2001)

Kennedy, P., *Evenings in the Duffrey* (McGlashan & Gill, Dublin, 1875)

King, J. and Joly, J. R., *The case of John Atherton, Bishop of Waterford in Ireland: fairly represented: Against a late partial edition of Dr. Barnard's relation, and sermon at his funeral. … with a brief account of a conspiracy against the life of Mr. Robert Hawkins, Minister of Chilton, Bucks … also of the plot of Robert Young, and S. Blackhead, against the Bishop of Rochester* (Luke Stokoe, London, 1710)

Knapp, A. and Baldwin, W. (eds), *Newgate Calendar* (J. Robins & Co., London, 1824)

Le Fanu, J. S., *The Cock and Anchor* (William Curry, Dublin, 1845)

Lee, G. A., *Leper Hospitals in Medieval Ireland* (Four Courts Press, Dublin, 1996)

Lewis, S., *A Topographical Dictionary of Ireland* (S. Lewis & Co., London, 1837)

Luddy, M., *Prostitution and Irish Society, 1800–1940* (Cambridge University Press, Cambridge, 2007)

Lyons, J. B., *The Quality of Mercer's: The Story of Mercer's Hospital 1734–1991* (Glendale, Dublin, 1991)

Lyons, Mary (ed.), *Memoirs of Mrs Margaret Leeson* (The Lilliput Press, Dublin, 1995)

Madden, R. R., *The United Irishmen: Their Lives and Times* (The Catholic Bookselling and Publishing Co., Dublin, 1860)

Maxwell, C., *Dublin under the Georges* (G.G. Harrap, London, 1946)

Maxwell, C., *The Stranger in Ireland: From the Reign of Elizabeth to the Great Famine* (Cape, London, 1954)

McCabe, D., *St Stephen's Green, Dublin, 1660–1875* (The Stationery Office, Dublin, 2011)

McCall, P. J., *In the Shadow of St Patrick's* (Sealy, Bryers & Walker, Dublin, 1894)

McCready, C. T., *Dublin Street Names, Dated and Explained* (Hodges Figgis & Co., Dublin, 1892)

McGregor, J., *New Picture of Dublin* (W. Curry, Jun., Dublin, 1828)

Moore, G., *Parnell and His Island* (Swan, Sonnenschein, Lowrey & Co., Dublin, 1887)

O'Brien, E., *The Royal College of Surgeons in Ireland: 1784–1984* (Eason, Dublin, 1983)

O'Brien, J. V., *Dear, Dirty Dublin: A City in Distress, 1899–1916* (University of California Press, Berkeley, 1982)

O'Keefe, J., *Recollections of the Life of John O'Keeffe – Written by Himself* (Henry Colburn, London, 1826)

O'Reilly, Andrew, *Reminiscences of an Emigrant Milesian* (R. Bentley, London, 1853)

Porter, F. T., *Twenty Years' Recollections of an Irish Police Magistrate* (Hodges, Foster & Figgis, Dublin, 1880)

Sheridan, T., *The Poems of Thomas Sheridan*, ed. Robert Hogan (University of Delaware Press, New Jersey, 1994)

Sullivan, Timothy Daniel, *Speeches from the Dock* (M. H. Gill & Son, Dublin, 1953)

Usher, R., *Protestant Dublin, 1660–1760: Architecture and Iconography* (Palgrave, McMillan, New York, 2012)

Walsh, J. E., *Sketches of Ireland Sixty Years Ago* (J. McGlashan, London, 1847)

Warburton, J., Whitelaw, J. and Walsh, R., *History of the City of Dublin* (W. Bulmer & Co. London, 1818)

Ward, M., *Hannah Sheehy Skeffington, Suffragette and Sinn Féiner* (UCD Press, Dublin, 2017)

Whaley, T. and Sullivan, E., *Buck Whaley's Memoirs* (De La More Press, London, 1906)

Widdess, J., *A Dublin School of Medicine and Surgery: An account of the Schools of Surgery, Royal College of Surgeons, Dublin: 1789–1948; a Dublin school of medicine and surgery* (E. & S. Livingstone, Edinburgh, 1949)

Wright, G. N., *An Historical Guide to Ancient and Modern Dublin* (Baldwin, Cradock and Joy, London, 1821)

OFFICIAL REPORTS

Great Britain. Parliament. House of Commons. *(1882). Report from the select committee on contagious diseases acts: Together with the proceedings of the committee, minutes of evidence and appendix* (London, 1882)

NEWSPAPERS AND PERIODICALS

Cork Constitution

Derby Mercury

Dublin Courant

Daily Express (Dublin)

Dublin Evening Post

Dublin Morning Register

Dublin Intelligence

Dublin Mercantile Advertiser

Hibernian Journal

Ipswich Journal

Irish Builder & Engineer

Irish Ecclesiastical Record

Pue's Occurrences

The Drogheda Argus and Leinster Journal

The Fitzwilliam Post

The Freeman's Journal

The Irish Press

The Irish Times

The Lancet

The Pilot

The Times (London)

Saunders's News-Letter

Waterford Mail

Whalley's Newsletter

ARTICLES

Butler, Beatrice Bayley, 'Lady Arabella Denny, 1707–1792', *Dublin Historical Record*, Vol. 9, No. 1 (1946), pp. 1–20. Available on JSTOR: www.jstor.org/stable/30079325

Maguire, M., 'The organisation and activism of Dublin's Protestant working class, 1883–1935', *Irish Historical Studies*, Vol. XXIX, No. 13 (May 1994)

ONLINE

www.bureauofmilitaryhistory.ie

www.rcpi.ie

ACKNOWLEDGEMENTS

Digging out interesting material for a book such as this one is largely a solitary business, but it could never happen without the help of the hardworking staff of Dublin's repositories and libraries. Thanks as usual are due to the staff at the National Library of Ireland and the National Archives. I'm particularly grateful to the staff at the Irish Architectural Archive in Merrion Square. Big thanks are also due to Paul Reynolds for the photographs.

I'd also like to thank Patrick O'Donoghue, who came up with the idea for the book, Noel O'Regan for his patience and work on the text, and the rest of the staff at Mercier Press for their insight and encouragement during the process. As usual, a book like this couldn't happen without the co-operation of my family, who take up the slack at home while I'm off enjoying myself in dusty libraries, so thanks to Nóirín, Róisín, Ella and Jack for putting up with me during the process. On a personal level I'd like to thank Mícheál Ó Doibhilín, publisher of *Kilmainham Tales* and the only Dublin man I know to have had a curry named after him, for the many pleasurable hours discussing misery, death and hanging among other matters. Thanks also to fellow 'culture club' members Mary, Kevin and Anton for letting me test-drive some of the stories on them and to Dave Kelly and the Dublin Currach Rowers Union for providing a bit of sanity and encouragement when it was most needed.

Finally, I'd like to dedicate this book to the memory of the chairman of the culture club, 'The Blue Panther' Anton O'Toole – a man who was only too happy to put me straight on a few matters concerning the history of Dublin.